◄SPEARHEA

7TH FLIEGER DIVISION
Student's Fallschirmjäger Elite

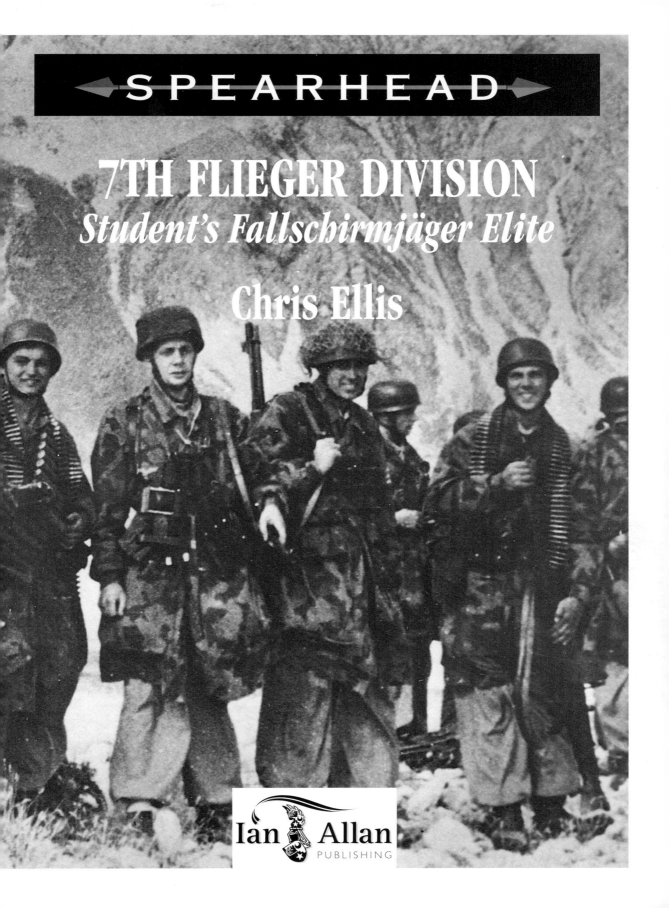

SPEARHEAD

7TH FLIEGER DIVISION
Student's Fallschirmjäger Elite

Chris Ellis

Ian Allan
PUBLISHING

First published 2002

ISBN 0 7110 2855 9

© Compendium Publishing 2002

Published by Ian Allan Publishing

an imprint of Ian Allan Publishing Ltd, Hersham, Surrey KT12 4RG.
Printed by Ian Allan Printing Ltd, Hersham, Surrey KT12 4RG.

Code: 0201/A2

British Library Cataloguing in Publication Data
A CIP catalogue record for this book is available from the British Library

Editor: Donald Sommerville
Design: Compendium Design
Illustrations: Mark Franklin

Cover: Fallschirmjäger at Cassino. TRH Pictures

Previous page: Well-armed paratroops during the
Gran Sasso raid. (All photos Chris Ellis collection,
unless credited otherwise.)

Abbreviations

AA	Anti-aircraft		battalion, where indicated,	Maint	Maintenance
AB	Airborne		takes the form of a Roman	MC	Motorcycle
Amb	Ambulance		numeral, thus II./FJR 2,	Med	Medium or
Arty	Artillery		indicating 2nd Battalion,		Medical
asst	Assistant		2nd Parachute Regiment	MG	Machine gun
A/Tk	Anti-tank	FJD	Fallschirmjäger-Division	Mor	Mortar
Bn	Battalion		(parachute division). The	Mot Inf	Motorised infantry
BR	British		divisional number takes the	MP	Military Police
Brig	Brigade		form of a prefix, thus 4. FJD	QM	Quartermaster
Bty	Battery		for 4th Parachute Division	Pl	Platoon
camo	camouflage	FlaRegt	Flak Regiment	PzJg	Panzerjäger (anti-tank)
Cav	Cavalry	FPzD	'HG' Fallschirm-Panzer-Division	Recce	Reconnaissance
CC	Combat Command		'Hermann Göring'	RA	Royal Artillery
C-in-C	Commander-in-Chief	gren	Grenade	RHQ	Regimental HQ
Col	Column	HMG	Heavy MG	RZ	as in RZ20 parachute—
Coy	Company	Hy	Heavy		*Rückenpackung Zwangaulösung,*
Det	Detachment	Inf	Infantry		lit backpack delivery system
DZ	Dropzone	LLStR	Luftland-Sturm-Regiment	Sect	Section
ea	each		(air-landing assault	Sig	Signals
Engr	Engineer		regiment), with a battalion	SP	Self-propelled
FA	Field Artillery		prefix as before, thus	Tac	Tactical
FJR	Fallschirmjäger-regiment		II./LLStR	Tk	Tank
	(parachute regiment). This	LMG	Light MG	Veh	Vehicle
	may be followed by the	Lt	light		
	number of the regiment,	Lt	Lieutenant	**Dates**	
	thus FJR 2. The individual	LZ	Landing zone	20/7/54	20 July 1954

CONTENTS

1 Origins & History 6

2 Ready For War 12

3 In Action 18

4 Equipment & Markings 68

5 People 82

6 Postwar 88

7 Assessment 90

8 Reference 92

Index 96

The German airborne troops of World War 2 were one of the legendary fighting forces of that epic period, still well recognised from those days even by younger generations born years afterwards. The spectacular air drops in Belgium and Holland in 1940, then a new and previously unheard of element of the 'Blitzkrieg' type of warfare, had an impact of fear and alarm which was rather more effective than some of the actual military results achived. The imagery of hundreds of soldiers parachuting into action from swarms of aircraft was a type of warfare that not even science fiction writers had envisaged. And the sharp new functional combat dress they wore was fearful and alarming compared to service dress anyone had seen before. Old newsreels of German parachute landings in 1940 in war history ducumentaries still thrill and capture the imagination when seen today. The German parachute operations of 1940 had an influence on British defence attitudes and preparations when Britain was next, in theory, in line to be invaded. And the German airborne activities also caused both the British and United States armies to raise their own airborne forces in 1941-42, largely based on the the German example and ideas. But as this book shows, there were limitations to the value of airborne operations, even for the pioneers of this type of warfare.

Acknowledgements
For help with photographs, organisation charts, and information to supplement my own references, I extend my thanks to Peter Chamberlain and Simon and George Forty.

Chris Ellis
November 2001

ORIGINS & HISTORY

Wild notions of flying soldiers into battle were put forward as fantasies over the centuries, long before man had actually mastered the idea of flight. One of the ideas portrayed in patriotic French prints when Napoleon threatened to invade England in the early 1800s was a force of soldiers carried over the English Channel in hot air balloons to supplement the soldiers arriving by sea and through a hastily dug Channel Tunnel! Far fetched as these notions were – in this case assuming an adequate supply of balloons and an obliging wind – it is clear that utilising the sky and aerial transport as a means of carrying war to the enemy was occupying military minds from quite early times. When balloons became a practical possibility they were used by the military in, for example, the American Civil War and some colonial wars as an aid to military reconnaissance, even though they had no direct offensive capability.

By the time of World War I with its military airships and aeroplanes, however, the parachute had been perfected, as an escape aid from damaged aircraft and balloons, and the first real suggesion of using soldiers landed by parachute was almost certainly put forward by the ever-inventive Brigadier-General Billy Mitchell, one of the US Army's pioneer flyers. Noting the stalemate on the Western Front when the United States entered the war, he proposed that one way to make a breakthrough would be to land battalions by parachute behind enemy lines. The problem here was the fact that training a number of infantry battalions to land by parachute, and to get together enough parachutes to equip them and enough aircraft to carry them would be an immense logistic problem that would take a minimum of six months to achieve. But this was 1918 and the war ended in November of that year with no decisions being taken over this very prescient scheme.

In the 1920s the Italian Army carried out some trial drops with parachutists but did not pursue the idea. It was the Russians who developed the idea of military airborne operations in a big way. In the 1920s the Soviet government supported and funded sport parachuting, both from aircraft and from specially built jumping towers. It was popular and keenly followed, with the Osswiachim Parachute Club as national organiser. By 1940 there were over a thousand town and village parachute clubs affiliated to the national organisation. Against this background the first Red Army parachute units were formed experimentally in 1928. The first recorded use of parachute forces in the Red Army was in the military exercises of 1930 when a platoon commanded by a lieutenant dropped south of Moscow and 'captured' a divisional HQ with all its staff. The first Red Army parachute brigade was formed in 1932, 400 strong, and this force made demonstration drops at the Moscow Air Days of 1933 and 1934. By 1935 this force had been greatly expanded and in the summer exercises of that year, near Kiev, there was a drop by 1,000 parachute troops, followed by 5,000 airborne troops flown into the drop zone by transport aircraft. Official photographs and newsreel film of this spectacular event made some impact in the West as previous activities had not been publicised by the secretive Russians. A similar demonstration involving 6,000 airborne troops was staged in the 1936 summer exercises near Minsk in the Ukraine and this time military observers were invited from Britain, France and Czechoslovakia, and on this occasion they also witnessed the airborne forces going into action with conventional infantry weapons immediately after landing. Leading the British observers was Major-General Archibald Wavell, and his report of the event included the oft-quoted remark, 'If I had not seen it for myself, I should not have believed such a thing to be possible.'

By this time the Red Army was also experimenting with air drops of artillery and light vehicles, and was also looking at the use of gliders to land infantry and equipment. All this experience and development was dissipated, however, in 1937 when Stalin began his infamous purge of the army high command. Among the victims was Marshal Mikhail Tukhachevski, the dynamic C-in-C of the Red Army who had enthusiastically sanctioned and sponsored the establishment and growth of the airborne forces. The Parachute Command was disbanded and the troops dispersed to ordinary units. It was 1941 before the Red Army once again established airborne forces.

GERMAN INTEREST

The German high command was clearly aware of developments in Russia. Even before the Nazi Party came to power the old Weimar Republic's Reichswehr (armed forces) had a secret agreement with the Soviet government throughout the 1920s and early 1930s whereby weapons development and training was carried out covertly in Russia as a means of overcoming the strict conditions of the 1919 Versailles Treaty. One of a number of staff officers who travelled and worked in Russia in this period was Major Kurt Student who had been a flying ace and squadron commander in the Imperial Air Force of 1916–18. At this time Student was mainly concerned with engine and aircraft development but his brief covered all matters related to air operations.

Student was not the instigator of airborne operations in the German armed forces, however, being too junior in rank when the Nazi Party came to power in early 1933. A Reichs Aviation Ministry was set up in 1933 and Student, now an Oberstleutnant (lt-col) was appointed to take charge of technical training schools. Gliding and flying clubs were initially used to build up a cadre of trained personnel for the embryonic Luftwaffe (air force). Erhard Milch, a former director of Lufthansa, was appointed as aviation secretary to oversee the build up, with Hermann Göring in political control as Reichskommissar for Air. It was not until March 1935 that the Luftwaffe's formation was officially announced by which time it already had over 1,800 aircraft and 20,000 men, all in contravention of the terms of the Versailles Treaty. Göring now became formally commander of the Luftwaffe and the chief of staff was General Walther Wever (transferred from the Army) who was an astute and hard-working staff officer, though he was killed in an air accident in May 1936 and replaced by General Albert Kesselring. It was Wever who suggested to Göring – sceptical at first – that a battalion of parachute troops should be formed by the Luftwaffe, and it was Wever who kept the initial momentum going and ensured funding for training and equipment.

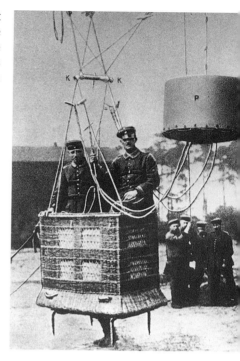

Above: The earliest use of parachutes was during WWI for escaping from damaged observation balloons.

The first men to become German parachute troops were not, however, Luftwaffe or even Army men; they were para-military policemen. This was due to Göring's influence and position of power. As Minister-President of Prussia, among his many offices, he was also the head of the Prussian Landespolizei. This was a para-military organisation of armed police which had been formed in Weimar days as a means of flouting the Versailles Treaty and putting more men under arms than was possible through the limited size permitted to the Heer (Army). At the time the Luftwaffe was formally announced in March 1935 other elements of re-organisation transferred all the para-military police units to the Army, and civilian policing was left to local forces of conventional type. Göring enjoyed sufficient power to retain direct control of one unit, Landespolizeigruppe *General Göring*, ostensibly to protect his own office and activities as a sort of private bodyguard. This was also transferred to the Army on 1 April 1935, and was renamed the Regiment *General Göring* while retaining its same duties. When General Wever persuaded Göring that a German parachute force was desirable to match Red Army progress, Göring selected his elite regiment to form the nucleus. In September 1935 he passed a formal order to Oberstleutnant Jakoby, the regimental commander stating that: 'The regiment will be transferred on 1 October 1935, intact, into the Luftwaffe. From volunteers of the Regiment you will organise a Paratroop Battalion as a cadre for the future German Parachute Troops.'

During October the regiment moved to the Altengrabow training area to familiarise themselves with aircraft and parachutes. From there they moved to the Döbritz training area and at Jüterbog airfield they lined up to watch a demonstration jump by a corporal with parachute experience. He made a heavy landing, due to misjudgement, and was carried away unconscious. However, this did not stop over 600 men coming forward next day when volunteers were called for to form the first parachute battalion. Named 1. Bataillon (1st Battalion), Regiment *General Göring*, the commander was Major Bruno Bräuer and the adjutant was Oberleutnant Vogel. The company commanders were Hauptmann Reinburger and Oberleutnants Kroh, Schulz, and Walther. All of them were soon promoted and all went on to important commands in World War II. Later the battalion was redesignated as the 4. Bataillon, Regiment *General Göring*, though it changed again to 1. Bataillon, Fallschirmjäger-Regiment 1 (1st Battalion, 1st Parachute Regiment), when the parachute forces were re-organised into 7. Flieger-Division in 1938.

Before then, however, there were more developments. Early in 1936 a Luftwaffe Parachute School was set up at Stendal, 60km north of Magdeburg, and this also became the official garrison town of the new parachute forces. Initially, of course, the 1st Battalion formed the entire establishment. They got down to serious training and the development of equipment, including the first standardised static-line parachute, designated RZ1. Techniques for delivering paratroops from the Junkers Ju 52 transport were tried and valuable work was done. However, there was a lull in expansion of the new force after its mentor, General Wever, was killed in an air crash. His successor, Kesselring, preferred to concentrate on expanding the air fleet and regarded paratroops as a sideline. However, by this time Kurt Student, now a colonel (Oberst), had been appointed Inspector General for Luftwaffe Training Schools, and the Stendal Parachute School came within his province.

The first official appearance of the Luftwaffe paratroops was in October 1936 when a platoon was dropped into simulated action during the autumn exercises that took place in Lower Saxony. By this time the German Army, too, was giving serious thought to paratroop formations and received permission to organise a

parachute company. This was formed early in 1937 and sent to Stendal to train since the Army had no parachute training facilities of its own. The company commander was Oberleutnant Zahn and his second-in-command was Oberleutnant Pelz, noted at the time as a leading pentathlon exponent. By the autumn of 1937 this company was considered fully trained and also had a full complement of heavy weapons. In the spring of 1937 the Luftwaffe parachute battalion and the new Army parachute company jumped in exercises at Mecklenburg observed by Hitler, who was said to be impressed by the spectacle. It was now decided to expand the Army parachute company to battalion strength and this was completed by the spring of 1938. The first battalion commander was Major Heidrich, an experienced infantry instructor who went to Stendal to qualify as a parachutist first despite being then aged 41. This followed the example set by Major Bruno Bräuer of the Regiment *General Göring* who also qualified as soon as he was appointed and had then made the first 'official' jump of the new German parachute arm two years earlier on 11 May 1936.

Above: Balloon parachutists during WWI. Parachutes were developed as aids to escape damaged aircraft and balloons. Observation balloons were extensively used by the military from the American Civil War onwards by all leading powers, including the Germans. This was an early appreciation of the value of airpower to further military operations, giving a third dimension to the land war.

7. FLIEGER IS FORMED

By the spring of 1938 Hitler's ambitions for expanding 'Greater Germany' were well under way, starting with a covert plan to annexe Czechoslovakia, finalised as Fall Grün (Case Green) in May. This necessitated some hasty military planning and the use of airborne troops was seen as a way of getting behind the strong Czech border defences. To organise the airborne arm from the forces already available, the experienced Kurt Student was appointed with the rank of Generalmajor and in the way the Luftwaffe had of designating their air combat commands, the Luftwaffe

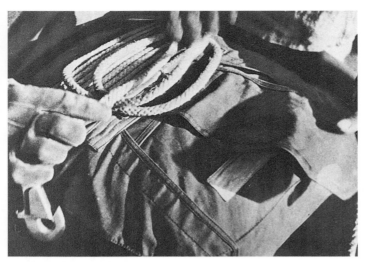

Above: Detail showing the static line on an RZ1 parachute, the original German parachute that was superseded by the RZ20.

airborne forces became 7. Flieger-Division from 1 July 1938, and Student's command became effective from that date. However, he had to work fast because the division was required to be combat-ready by 15 September in time for Case Green to start. Student, enthusiastic and hard-working was up to the task, which was why he had been selected, but he also had the advantage of commanding Göring's respect and confidence which allowed him to plan, train, and organise in the way he thought best. This freedom of action was almost certainly helped by the fact that at the time nobody else of high rank knew anything about the subject!

Student set up his divisional HQ at Berlin-Tempelhof airfield with Hauptmann Heinz Trettner as chief of staff and a small planning team picked from trusted Luftwaffe colleagues. Such directives on airborne operations that had by then emanated from the Armed Forces High Command (OKW) saw the use of paratroops largely for securing airfields to allow the Luftwaffe to fly in troops, or sabotage or raiding operations in small units behind enemy lines. Student started planning afresh, however. His conception was that airborne operations would ideally take place in three phases. First would be the landing of shock troops by glider to take out key positions and defence posts. Secondly paratroops would secure airfields or areas big enough to land aircraft, or attack defence lines from the rear. Thirdly air landing troops would be brought in to the landing zones already secured by the paratroops to pave the way for the arrival of regualr infantry and heavy weapons. Student described these as shock tactics deliberately intended to cause 'surprise, fright and panic' combined with speed of events.

For the Case Green operations the Army parachute battalion was taken under command of 7. Flieger. At the time the division comprised Division HQ; 1st Battalion of 1. FJR (Oberstleutnant Bräuer), the Army Parachute Infantry Battalion (Major Heidrich), Air Landing Battalion 'Regiment *General Göring*' (Major Sydow), an infantry gun company (Oberleutnant Schram), a medical company and a signals company. Also included was a newly formed glider company commanded by Leutnant Weiss. This was equipped with the new DFS 230 glider which had been ordered in 1937 after a demonstration in front of Kesselring, Milch, Udet and other senior Luftwaffe officers. The famous test pilot Hanna Reitsch had flown the prototype on that occasion and impressed the watchers with her fast precise landing from a 1,000m cast-off by the towing Ju 52. Eight soldiers demonstrated a fast exit from the aircraft. All other tests were successful and a small initial order was placed.

The DFS 230 had been designed in 1933 for meteorological research but when the influential aviator Ernst Udet saw it he recognised its potential as a load or personnel carrier for military use and used his contacts to secure development of a sturdier military prototype. For Case Green six wings of Ju 52s were put under command, but the division was still short of men for the air landing component and the Army could not be persuaded to put more units under Luftwaffe control. To make up the numbers Student asked Göring if the Nazi Party's top SA unit, the Regiment *Feldherrenhalle*, could be assigned and quickly be given some field training. This was done, though its fighting value would have been doubtful had the invasion of Czechoslovakia gone ahead.

Göring, with his SA rank and connections, was honorary colonel of the *Feldherrenhalle* and during the military element of their training, some young members of this SA regiment were given parachute and airborne experience and the regiment was affiliated to the Luftwaffe to the extent that the men wore Luftwaffe field dress when on annual manoeuvres. By this connection the regiment became, in effect, a reserve Luftwaffe unit and as soon as the war started the *Feldherrenhalle* members were absorbed into the air landing assault battalion and the new 2nd Parachute Regiment of the expanding 7. Flieger-Division. Others went to the Army's *Feldherrenhalle* Battalion.

Student and his men worked hard and he was able to report 7. Flieger 'combat ready' on 1 September 1938, two weeks ahead of the deadline. These two weeks were used for intensive air landing exercises. However, as is well-known, Case Green never took place, for the crisis talks that led to the Munich Agreement at the end of September resulted in Hitler being allowed to take over the German-speaking Sudetenland area of Czechoslovakia in October 1938 and war was averted for another year. Göring was keen to show off the Luftwaffe's air landing capability, anyway, so as part of the Czech occupation he had 7. Flieger fly into the key area around Freudenthal (their Case Green objective in fact) using an impressive fleet of 242 Junkers 52s. This was actually more of a demonstration than a realistic exercise for there was no opposition and no critical time factor, and a good deal of showing off. But Göring liked what he saw and said afterwards, 'This business has a great future.'

This event gave a good deal of new impetus to the build-up of a Luftwaffe airborne force, and Student's stock was high. From 1 January 1939, the Army Parachute Battalion was transferred to the Luftwaffe (not without much arm-twisting by Göring) and it became the 2nd Battalion, FJR 1, still commanded by Major Heidrich. The Air Landing Battalion became the 3rd Battalion, FJR 1 (Mayor Sydow) and Bräuer now commanded the newly expanded regiment with the rank of Oberst (colonel). His place as 1st Battalion commander was taken by Major von Grazy. The Army agreed to commit the 22nd Infantry Division as the designated air landing component for future operations, essentially an ordinary infantry division which would be carried in by the Ju 52 transports and would train in this role. Moreover it agreed the division would come under 7. Flieger command in battle. During 1939 the establishment of 7. Flieger-Division expanded considerably with the addition of 7th Howitzer Battery, 7th Anti-Tank Company, 7th Intelligence Company, 7th Medical Company and smaller support and logistics units. Student was given extra responsibility by being appointed, additionally, as Inspector-General of Airborne Troops.

A highlight of 1939 was the appearance of 7. Flieger troops in Hitler's huge 50th birthday parade in Berlin under the command of Oberst Bräuer. They made a big visual impact, not only with the German people but with Germany's potential enemies. For, unlike all the units in parade dress, the parachute battalions wore full combat kit with their distinctive jump smocks, helmets, and slung rifles. They looked as though they meant business.

Above: Troops learning jumping posture on a training rig, showing splayed leg position (much like a modern skydiver).

Below: Awaiting their turn for practice, Fallschirmjäger at Stendal Parachute Training School.

READY FOR WAR

Above right: Members of the I./FJR 1 boarding a static aircraft to practice exiting the Ju 52 during early training in 1938. These were the original intake of recruits to the regiment and all were volunteers.

Below right: German Fallschirmjäger recruit jumping from a stationary plane during training.

In March 1939, in defiance of the terms of the Munich Agreement, Hitler seized the remainder of Czechoslovakia by military force. For this 7. Flieger-Division was detailed to drop on and secure Kbely Airport near Prague and to seize Hradcany Castle, the seat of government. But a day-long blizzard prevented flying operations and fast moving Army units took these objectives instead. When the weather cleared 7. Flieger did no more than fly into the airport which was already in German hands.

POLAND

Hitler's next ambition was to take Poland and covert plans were made to mass the military units involved near the German–Polish border. Mobilisation was ordered on 26 August 1939. For its part 7. Flieger-Division was to move by road convoy from its base in Berlin to Breslau (then the capital of German Silesia but now Wroclaw in Poland). While the troops were on the move on 1 September 1939, the invasion of Poland started. The men of 7. Flieger heard the news during a meal break on the Autobahn. The division's units were ordered to airfields near Breslau there to await operational orders for deployment as the high command saw fit. However, no airborne operations were actually carried out in the campaign.

Britain and France had declared war on Germany on 3 September when Hitler ignored their ultimatum to withdraw his forces from Poland but they could give no direct military help to Poland and, if anything, their involvement caused the campaign to be hastened. Fast moving panzer divisions, using the *Blitzkrieg* tactics which made such an impact in World War II, seized several objectives that were earmarked to be taken by 7. Flieger. These included Graudenz and the Vistula Bridge near Pulawy, but in each case the troops were in their Ju 52s on the runway when the operations were called off. Morale among the men dropped in the circumstances, but in mid-September they actually saw action. However, this was in a motorised infantry role, not as paratroops.

Their task was to seize and secure airfields between the Vistula and Bug Rivers to deny their use to Polish units, many of which had been cut-off or outflanked in the fast moving ground war. First contact with the enemy was on 14 September when the 3rd Battalion clashed with Polish units. Student himself was nearly captured when his staff car inadvertently drove through a Polish position. And on 24 September the 2nd Battalion had a particularly tough engagement that brought the division's first casualties of the war at Wola-Gulowska. First of several men to die was Feldwebel (sergeant) Mensch, a

Above: Paratroops under training having their parachute packs checked before a jump.

Below: German Fallschirmjäger dived from the aircraft rather than jumped.

popular and experienced NCO. The dead were buried in an old fort at Demblin.

Soon Poland capitulated and 7. Flieger carried out 'occupation' duties, guarding airfields and Luftwaffe HQs and sorting out prisoners, before being ordered back to Berlin in mid-October. The division's leaders were disappointed that their skills in air-landing were not needed, but on the other hand this preserved the surprise factor which would be better exploited in Hitler's plan to conquer Western Europe in 1940. This scheme, Fall Gelb (Case Yellow), was already being developed.

TACTICS AND EQUIPMENT

During the winter months the men of 7. Flieger trained hard, and in early 1940 they started specialist training for their key part in the campaign to come. By then they had already long worked out their modes of operation and developed the special equipment needed in parachute drops and air landings.

Very distinctive to the parachute troops was the combat dress which comprised high boots, a long smock, and a rimless close-fitting helmet, plus detachable knee-pads for wear when jumping. This general style of clothing was adopted with detail variations by the parachute troops of other countries later in the war.

In the very earliest days a conventional ripcord parachute was used, but this had the disadvantage that jumping had to be done from a great height, well above the minimum safe height of 200 metres (650ft) for this type of chute. A much lower jump height was considered vital for military operations and very quickly a static-line parachute was developed, designated RZ1 which allowed a jump height of around 120 metres (400ft). With the RZ1 the static line was hooked to a rail inside the aircraft and the parachute was automatically pulled open at a safe distance from the aircraft. Because the Germans adopted the old Salvatore parachute design, which attached to the harness above the small of the back, the parachutist could not reach and manipulate the shroud lines. Descent and direction were not controllable—unlike their British and US counterparts. In these conditions it was also difficult for German paras to 'spill' the wind and after landing the man could be dragged along the ground and injured if the chute was difficult to release. The jerk of the static line also caused the chute to swing in descent and the jumper could do virtually nothing to control this. To reduce swing in the air the German paratroops used a distinctive spread-eagled 'diving' position as they left the aircraft and maintained this in descent. They were taught to land face forward on all fours, hence the provision of the knee pads and also elbow pads, though not all men wore the latter. Winds stronger than 14mph meant the chutes were carried over a wide area and the preferred weather for a 'copybook' drop was light airs and calm which was an obvious operational limitation. Later parachute designs, such as the RZ16 of 1940 and RZ20 of 1941, were better-shaped and more stable, but never satisfactory.

Above: Landing training—the position accounts for the padding on uniform knee and elbow.

Because of the parachutes' limitations the parachutists' side arms and ammunition were dropped separately in parachute containers, colour coded for each unit, and carried under the wings of the drop aircraft. The parachutist himself jumped carrying a pistol with 20 rounds, benzedrine tablets, field dressing, some food (chocolate, biscuits, etc.) and a knife, all carried in the pockets of the smock. The knife could be used to cut away the parachute lines if there was difficulty releasing the harness. The necessity of using the arms and equipment containers was another limitation. Even though they had smoke markers which activated when they hit the ground, these containers still had to be collected, opened and the contents distributed, before the troops could go into action effectively. If the containers fell far away, got stuck in trees, or fell into streams, etc., there were major problems.

The standard paratroop carrier – and glider tug – was the slow but rugged tri-motor Junkers 52. It was designed as an airliner in 1930 and the first major user was, naturally, Lufthansa, though it was also sold abroad to other airlines such as Swissair, Air France and about 28 other airline customers. Militarised versions were ordered for the new Luftwaffe in 1934–35, mainly as transports. Though it was obsolescent by the late 1930s, with its fixed undercarriage, low top speed (270km/hr or 168mph), and limited capacity it remained in service through World War II. It was immensely tough and reliable and was popularly known to servicemen as 'Tante Ju' (Auntie Junkers). One aircraft could carry 13 paratroops sitting facing inwards on canvas seats. The exit door was in the port (left) side. A Staffel of 12 aircraft could carry a company of 156 men, and a Gruppe of four Staffeln could carry a battalion. This was 'rule of thumb' and in practice more aircraft were often used to carry support units or reinforcements, etc., and equipment such as light anti-tank guns and motorcycle combinations. Later it was found that these types of item could be carried under the fuselage between the wheel struts.

Parachute training lasted eight weeks and men were taught to pack their own parachutes. Much ground training was given in landing techniques and aircraft exit techniques using ground fuselage rigs and suitable jumping platforms and towers. Extensive physical training was given to make the soldier fit for the stress of jumping, landing and going into action and the German paratroops were some of the fittest and toughest fighting men of the war. This was aided by the fact that all were volunteers; any unfit or psychologically unsure men were weeded out early on in the training course. While Stendal remained the main training school for paratroops, further schools were opened during World War II at Wittstock, Braunschweig, and Châteaudun in France. This was necessary as the German parachute forces expanded greatly as the war progressed.

7. FLIEGER-DIVISION AS AT NOVEMBER 1938

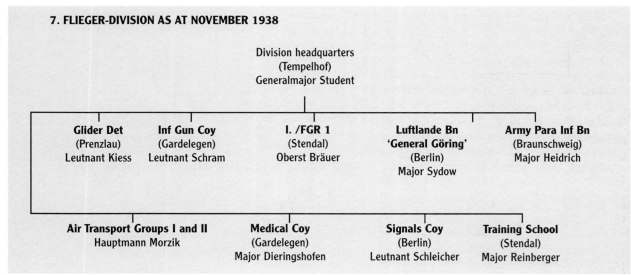

Division headquarters
(Tempelhof)
Generalmajor Student

Glider Det
(Prenzlau)
Leutnant Kiess

Inf Gun Coy
(Gardelegen)
Leutnant Schram

I. /FGR 1
(Stendal)
Oberst Bräuer

**Luftlande Bn
'General Göring'**
(Berlin)
Major Sydow

Army Para Inf Bn
(Braunschweig)
Major Heidrich

Air Transport Groups I and II
Hauptmann Morzik

Medical Coy
(Gardelegen)
Major Dieringshofen

Signals Coy
(Berlin)
Leutnant Schleicher

Training School
(Stendal)
Major Reinberger

Above: Order of battle of 7. Flieger Division at November 1938.

Right: Men of the 7. Flieger Division march past on Hitler's birthday parade, 20 April 1939.

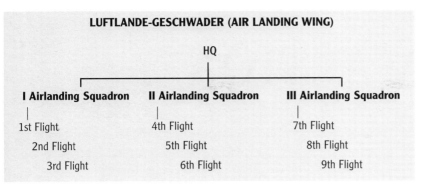

LUFTLANDE-GESCHWADER (AIR LANDING WING)

```
                            HQ
        ┌───────────────────┼───────────────────┐
I Airlanding Squadron  II Airlanding Squadron  III Airlanding Squadron
        │                   │                   │
   1st Flight           4th Flight          7th Flight
   2nd Flight           5th Flight          8th Flight
   3rd Flight           6th Flight          9th Flight
```

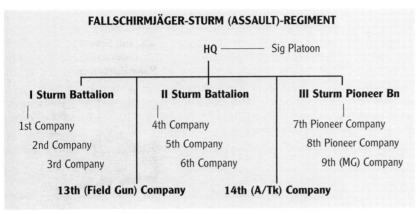

FALLSCHIRMJÄGER-STURM (ASSAULT)-REGIMENT

```
                    HQ ──────── Sig Platoon
        ┌───────────────────┼───────────────────┐
 I Sturm Battalion    II Sturm Battalion    III Sturm Pioneer Bn
        │                   │                   │
  1st Company          4th Company         7th Pioneer Company
  2nd Company          5th Company         8th Pioneer Company
  3rd Company          6th Company         9th (MG) Company

     13th (Field Gun) Company        14th (A/Tk) Company
```

Above left: Organisation of the Ju 52 Luftlande-Geschwader 1 used for para operations in 1940.

Left: German organisation chart dated September 1940 for the Fallschirmjäger-Sturmregiment. For the 1941 Crete operation a fourth battalion was added.

Below: Paratroop stick dropping from a Junkers Ju 52. This shows the correct intervals between jumpers in a stick.

IN ACTION

Above: Parachutes hanging up awaiting packing. The Fallschirmjäger packed his own parachute prior to jumping.

INVASION PLANS

Fall Gelb (Case Yellow), the invasion of France and Flanders, was decided upon by Hitler as soon as the Polish campaign was over. He issued orders on 9 October 1939 to commence the offensive in the West only a month later on 12 November, but the Army High Command was able to get it postponed, pointing out the logistic impossibility of moving the divisions from Poland to the West, then reorganising them for the new campaign, all against the background of worsening winter weather. Therefore the campaign was put back to spring 1940.

One of the uses for the airborne forces, already decided on, was the taking of key positions in the forthcoming offensive, and to prepare for this Student set up a unit under the 'camouflage' name of Test Section Friedrichshafen. This unit comprised the 1st Company of the 1st Battalion, FJR 1, and the Pioneer Platoon of the 2nd Battalion, plus a glider squadron, all under command of Hauptmann Koch. The force totalled 11 officers and 427 men. Their task was to perfect the technique of landing gliders in the smallest possible area with a dedicated assault force. Later this unit revealed its true purpose when it was renamed Assault Battalion *Koch* (Stürmabteilung *Koch*).

This was all part of the preparation for the deployment of 7. Flieger in the opening stages of the forthcoming offensive. The assault battalion would take the key Belgian frontier fort of Eben Emael, a commanding defence position, plus the key bridges along the Albert Canal. The rest of 7. Flieger, with 22nd Air Landing Division under command also, would take and secure the key airfields and river crossings in Holland. For this campaign 7. Flieger was put under the nominal control of Luftflotte 2 (commanded by Kesselring) which would be providing the air cover for the operation.

ACTION IN NORWAY AND DENMARK

The first parachute operation of the war took place not as part of the planned Case Yellow, but as part of Operation Weserübung (Weser Exercise), the occupation of Norway and Denmark. This operation had to be organised and staged hurriedly as the Germans got wind of a planned Anglo–French landing in Norway to block the shipping of iron ore to Germany from northern Sweden which was taken out from Narvik, down the Norwegian coast to the Baltic ports. To forestall Allied plans, German forces moved into Denmark and Norway on the morning of 9 April 1940.

THE AIR LANDING CORPS (LUFTLANDEKORPS) AS AT 10 MAY 1940

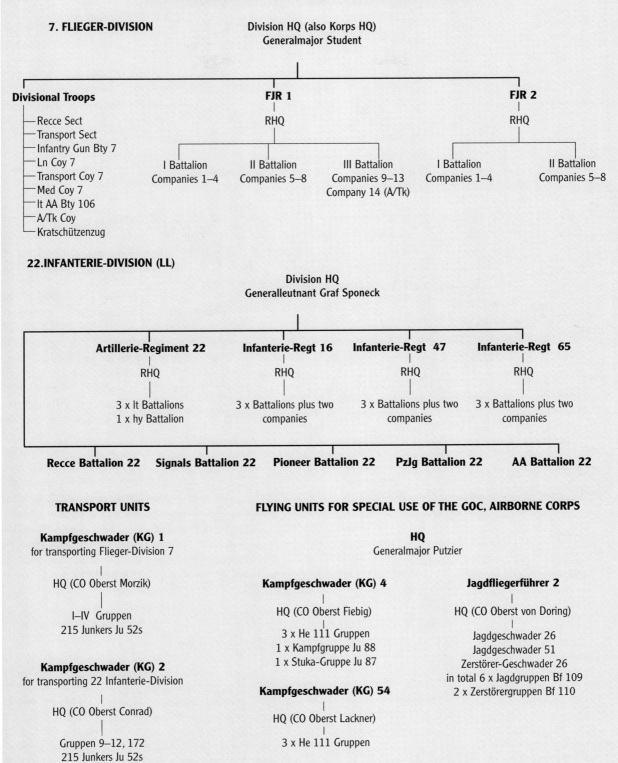

7. FLIEGER-DIVISION

Division HQ (also Korps HQ)
Generalmajor Student

Divisional Troops
— Recce Sect
— Transport Sect
— Infantry Gun Bty 7
— Ln Coy 7
— Transport Coy 7
— Med Coy 7
— lt AA Bty 106
— A/Tk Coy
— Kratschützenzug

FJR 1
RHQ

I Battalion
Companies 1–4

II Battalion
Companies 5–8

III Battalion
Companies 9–13
Company 14 (A/Tk)

FJR 2
RHQ

I Battalion
Companies 1–4

II Battalion
Companies 5–8

22.INFANTERIE-DIVISION (LL)

Division HQ
Generalleutnant Graf Sponeck

Artillerie-Regiment 22
RHQ

3 x lt Battalions
1 x hy Battalion

Infanterie-Regt 16
RHQ

3 x Battalions plus two
companies

Infanterie-Regt 47
RHQ

3 x Battalions plus two
companies

Infanterie-Regt 65
RHQ

3 x Battalions plus two
companies

Recce Battalion 22 **Signals Battalion 22** **Pioneer Battalion 22** **PzJg Battalion 22** **AA Battalion 22**

TRANSPORT UNITS

Kampfgeschwader (KG) 1
for transporting Flieger-Division 7

HQ (CO Oberst Morzik)

I–IV Gruppen
215 Junkers Ju 52s

Kampfgeschwader (KG) 2
for transporting 22 Infanterie-Division

HQ (CO Oberst Conrad)

Gruppen 9–12, 172
215 Junkers Ju 52s

FLYING UNITS FOR SPECIAL USE OF THE GOC, AIRBORNE CORPS

HQ
Generalmajor Putzier

Kampfgeschwader (KG) 4

HQ (CO Oberst Fiebig)

3 x He 111 Gruppen
1 x Kampfgruppe Ju 88
1 x Stuka-Gruppe Ju 87

Kampfgeschwader (KG) 54

HQ (CO Oberst Lackner)

3 x He 111 Gruppen

Jagdfliegerführer 2

HQ (CO Oberst von Doring)

Jagdgeschwader 26
Jagdgeschwader 51
Zerstörer-Geschwader 26
in total 6 x Jagdgruppen Bf 109
2 x Zerstörergruppen Bf 110

Map showing Fallschirmjäger deployments in the early war years, 1940–42.

Norway and Denmark: Parachute and air landings April 1940, including I./FJR 1 reinforcement of Narvik.

Holland: Airfields and bridges 10 May 1940.

Belgium: Fort Eben Emael and Albert Canal bridges 10 May 1940.

Corinth: Glider and paratroop landings on canal 27 April 1941.

Crete: Landings by 7. Flieger Division, 5. Gebirgs Division, Fallschirm Assault Regiment, Fallschirm-Pioneer-Bn, Corps Troops.

Eastern Front: 7. Flieger Division detachment and Div HQ.

Western Desert: Fallschirmjäger Brigade Ramcke November 1942.

Tunisia: Defensive ops 1942–43 by FJR 5 and Fallschirm-Pioneer-Bn 21.

Map showing Fallschirmjäger deployments in the later war years, 1943–45.

Leros: I./FJR 2, 12 November 1943.

Sicily: Defensive operations by 1. FJD, July 1943.

Italy, Anzio and Monte Cassino: Defensive operations by 1. FJD, 1943.

Italy, Rome: Defensive operations by 2. FJD, 1943.

Italy, Mt Rotondo: Capture of Italian Army HQ by II./FJR 6, September 1943.

Elba: Capture of island by II./FJR 7, 17 September 1943 .

Italy, Gran Sasso: Battlegroup Rescue of Mussolini, 12 September 1943.

Italy: Defensive operations in north by 4. FJD, 1944.

Western Front: Defence of Normandy and Brittany by 1. Fallschirm-Armee from July 1944.

Western Front: Defence of Maas and Waal rivers, September 1944.

Western Front: Ardennes Offensive, December 1944/January 1945.

Western Front: Defence of the Rhineland, 1945.

Eastern Front: 2. FJD at Zhitomir and Kirovgrad.

Eastern Front: 'Hermann Göring' Fallschirm-Pz-Korps defence of Breslau, 1945.

Eastern Front: Defence of Austria 1945.

Eastern Front: Defence of Berlin 9.FJD, 1945.

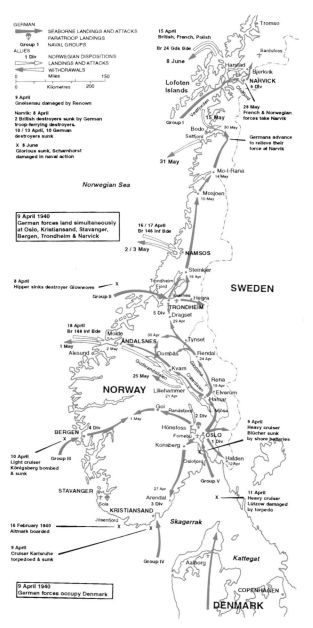

Above: The Battle of Norway.

Above right: Men of the 7. Flieger Division march past on Hitler's birthday parade, 20 April 1939. The collar and tie plus full parachute harness were normal for ceremonial occasions. A Luftwaffe general in ceremonial dress stands second in the line of officers nearest the camera.

Below right: Muster of Fallschirmjäger at Bjornfjell Station near Narvik. The CO in the foreground, Fritz Becker, is addressing his men.

To spearhead the Denmark operation, 1st Battalion of 1st Parachute Regiment (I./FJR 1) was deployed, commanded by Major Erich Walther. The 4th Company (less one platoon) was dropped on the Storstrøm causeway and Vordingborg bridge linking Falster and Seeland with Copenhagen, charged with holding it until the invading German divisions arrived to cross it. This they did in a copybook landing, and the few Danish troops holding the bridge were so surprised by the novelty of the event that they surrendered at once. Notice of this operation was so short that Hauptmann Walther Gericke, the company commander, had only a road map and postcards as a planning guide. The detached platoon was dropped on two airfields at Ålborg in northern Denmark to secure them for the air-landing troops and covering fighters. The operation was completed in 30 minutes.

The Battalion HQ and 2nd Company (Hauptmann Walther) were to land directly by aircraft at Fornebu airport, near Oslo, and secure it for 163rd Infantry Division to be flown in. This mission was nearly a disaster. The airport was obscured by fog and there was brisk AA fire from the Norwegian defenders. The Junkers 52s carrying the paratroops were forced to hold off and two of them collided. The situation was saved by one of the Bf 109 escorting fighters that ran out of fuel and force-landed on the runway firing its guns as it came in. Meanwhile the main force of Ju 52s carrying the infantry division had arrived and, seeing a gap in the fog, followed the Messerschmitt in, only to come under fire on the ground. By now, however, the Ju 52s carrying the paratroops had landed under cover of this diversion, and in 30 minutes they secured the airfield, as the defenders began to run out of ammunition and were overwhelmed by superior numbers. By evening all of Oslo was in German hands.

The 3rd Company (Leutnant von Brandis) was to secure Sola airport at Stavanger and, again, it was lucky to succeed for very murky weather and high winds made the drop zone hard to find. At one point the cloud base was as low as 10 metres (30ft). However, just as the aircraft approached they found a calm and clear patch over the airfield and the men dropped in copybook manner. A foretaste

of future problems came when the defenders at the edge of the airfield put down accurate small arms fire and prevented the paratroops from recovering their small arms and ammunition containers for over 30 minutes. Only the diversion when the follow-up Ju 52s with the air-landing troops arrived over the airfield allowed the situation to be retrieved and the paratroops swiftly secured the perimeter.

The 1st Company (Leutnant Schmidt) was held in reserve on 9 April, but on 14 April it, too, was deployed. On that evening it was dropped at Dombås in the Gudbrandsdal valley about 90 miles north of Oslo; this was such a disastrous operation that it was not publicised afterwards. The object was to hold the Trondheim–Lillehammer road south of Åndalsnes to prevent a newly landed British infantry brigade from linking up with Norwegian troops retreating north from Oslo. One Ju 52 was shot down on its approach run up the valley, and the other aircraft were too low, finding height difficult to judge over deep snow. Many containers were lost in snow drifts and some men were injured, or even killed, by low hard landings. Norwegian troops, well concealed in the valley sides and familiar with the area, pinned down the company with fire. Only 61 men survived the jump and after five days hard fighting there were only 34 left when they ran out of food and ammunition and surrendered. Schmidt was badly injured early on by small arms fire but stayed in command throughout. For this he was awarded the Knight's Cross. The men were not in captivity for long because the Norwegians capitulated the following month. But this action demonstrated a problem that was to be repeated several more times in the years ahead – the limited period that paratroops could realistically hold a position before being relieved by the main force. Schmidt's tiny force did well to last as long as it did, blocking a key route.

Above: Men of Assault Group *Koch* after having been relieved at Eban Emael (note name on truck) leaving for Maastricht.

More tough fighting came in the far north at Narvik. Road links there were primitive at the best of times but in winter they were non-existent. General Dietl's 34. Gebirgs Division had landed by sea at Narvik but was now cut off by a successful British landing near the port, with good gunfire support from the strong Royal Navy force of ships in Narvik Fjord. The only way in was by air and all the surviving companies of I./FJR 1 were parachuted in as reinforcements in the last two weeks of May. This was done piecemeal over several days – the last drop as late as 29 May – since the Ju 52s had to fly the long haul north from Trondheim. This necessitated fitting long range tanks inside the fuselage so only a handful of paratroops could be carried at a time. In addition a number of mountain troops were given quick seven day courses at the parachute school at Stendal and were also parachuted in with the paratroops.

The fierce fighting at Narvik only ended when the British pulled out at the end of May 1940 due to the grave situation in France. On 8 June 1940, men of I./FJR 1 at last moved into Narvik against no opposition. At this moment the men of II./FJR 1 were en route to Trondheim from Oslo by train as further reinforcements for Narvik, but they were no longer needed. With operations in Norway at an end, all the FJR 1 men returned to Germany on the cruiser *Nürnberg*.

EBEN EMAEL

Fall Gelb (Case Yellow) – the invasion of France and Flanders scheduled for 10 May 1940 was an immense undertaking, and the German airborne forces had a key part in its launch. In the Army Group B sector, Sixth Army, commanded by Generaloberst von Reichenau, had to cross the River Maas and push back or penetrate the Belgian defenders while heading for Tirlemont and neutralising the well defended area around Louvain from the north. This section of the front was covered by 4th Panzer Division and 151st Infantry Regiment of XXVII Corps which were routed from Aachen, through Maastricht, and over the border into Belgium.

At this point the fortress of Eben Emael, between the River Maas and Albert Canal, dominated the approaches and would be a formidable obstacle for the invaders. It was on a 150ft high ridge, surrounded by anti-tank ditches, and bristled with guns. In addition to taking the fort it was vital to secure the bridges over the Albert Canal. It was for this key task – taking out Eben Emael and capturing the bridges intact – that Sturmabteilung *Koch* had been formed and highly trained at Hildesheim in conditions of great secrecy and security. Hitler took a close personal interest in all the planning for Fall Gelb and, according to Student, it was Hitler's idea to take Eben Emael by a glider landing on the roof. Student was at first dubious, but when he studied the detail he thought it was possible. Later he described it as the most original of Hitler's many ideas.

The biggest immediate problem was bringing a DFS 230 glider to an abrupt halt on the relatively small roof the fort. Trials were carried out by wrapping barbed wire round the landing skid but this made little difference. Eventually they settled on a serrated metal cladding on the skid that would dig in like a ploughshare as the glider landed. Many practice landings were needed, however, and rehearsals were carried out on former Czech defence bunkers on the Sudetenland borders. The Germans also managed to get plans of the fort from pre-war building contractors, so the exact size of the fort could be replicated for landing practice, and they knew the internal layout.

Assault Group *Koch* comprised 11 officers and 427 men, plus 42 DFS 230 glider pilots. For the operation of 10 May it was divided into four groups, code named Granite, Iron, Steel and Concrete. Of these the key unit was Assault Group Granite (Oberleutnant Witzig) for it was to take the fort itself, the key to the whole invasion plan. In this group were two officers, and 83 NCOs and men, all trained as combat engineers, plus 11 gliders and pilots. On 9 May Assault Group *Koch* moved to Cologne-Ostheim and Cologne-Butzweilerhof airfields, and at 04.30 on 10 May it took off for its objectives.

Granite had a tough job. The fort was garrisoned by 1,200 men, had twelve 75mm howitzers in casements, four more in armoured cupolas, and two 120mm howitzers in armoured cupolas. There were also seven AA guns and numerous machine gun posts, all on top of a fort that was roughly diamond shaped and about 900m x 800m (980yd x 875yd) in size. To destroy the guns and emplacements, the men had two sizes of special hollow-charge grenades, conventional explosives, flamethrowers and machine guns. En route to the target two gliders were lost. One was cast off prematurely by mistake, but the glider with Oberleutnant Witzig snapped its tow rope and landed in a field. In his absence Leutnant Delica and the senior NCO, Oberfeldwebel Wenzel, took charge of the force when the gliders swooped out of the dawn sky and landed perfectly on the Eben Emael fort roof at 05.32. Meanwhile, Witzig had commandeered a car and gone for help. He got another Ju 52 to tow the glider out of the field in which it had landed, and his glider finally set down on the fort roof at 08.30, three hours late but there nonetheless.

The men of Granite, some 55 in all, had actually knocked out most of the enemy guns within ten minutes of

The German attack on the West.

	BELGIAN & DUTCH FORWARD DEFENCES
	FORTRESS HOLLAND
	GERMAN ATTACKS, 10/13 MAY
	GERMAN AIRBORNE LANDINGS, 10 MAY
	MOVEMENT OF ALLIED FORCES, 10 MAY

landing and were then engaged in clearing the interior galleries and pinning down the defenders in a lively fire fight. Only one gun cupola had been ignored as it was thought to be ineffective. This was not the case, however, as the twin guns in it opened fire and pinned men down. Leutnant Delica called in a Stuka squadron by radio to bomb the cupola. They missed, but the intensity of the bombing caused the Belgians to cease using the cupola anyway. The fighting in the fort actually went on for a whole day, because it was full of tunnels, galleries and underground magazines, all of which had to be fought for. In addition Belgian troops made several unco-ordinated attacks on the fort from the north-west. It was not until 07.00 on 11 May that Group Granite was relieved. Out of the tiny force that landed, Granite had lost six men killed and 20 wounded, but had achieved a victory out of proportion to its tiny size.

The other assault groups had less dramatic but equally important objectives. Assault Group Steel (Oberleutnant Altmann and 112 men) landed its gliders near the Veldwezelt bridge right on time at 05.30, took the bridge in a brisk assault, and removed the explosives which had been set to blow it. They had a tough job holding the bridge, however, against heavy counter-attacks, and they called in Stukas to bomb the attackers. 4th Panzer Division was due to relieve them during the day, but did not arrive until the following afternoon on 11 May. Some relief came on the afternoon of 10 May, however, when men of 51st Engineer Battalion managed to cross the Maas and work their way up the banks of the canal towards the bridges.

Assault Group Concrete (Leutnant Schlacht and 134 men) landed at 05.15 and seized Vroenhoven bridge quickly, despite superior Belgian numbers. The Belgians had not stood to, thinking that the gliders were merely crashing aircraft. The bridge was saved from demolition by the initiative of Gefreiter (corporal) Stenzel who pulled the wires from the charge just as a Belgian engineer was about to detonate it. Numerous Belgian counter-attacks were beaten back and an artillery barrage which attempted to destroy the bridge proved ineffective. The group was finally relieved at 21.40 that evening when an infantry battalion arrived on the approach march from Maastricht. In the day's fighting, Concrete lost seven killed and 24 wounded.

The only failure was at the objective of Assault Group Iron (Leutnant Schächter and 114 men). The Canne bridge was near the Eben Emael fort and could be seen from there. As the force landed at 05.35 it was spotted by the fort commander who immediately blew the bridge. The men could be enfiladed from the fort and suffered heavy casualties of 22 dead and 26 injured. Schächter was killed and his deputy Leutnant Meissner took command. It was 23.30 before the bridgehead was relieved after tough fighting.

HOLLAND

The Army Group B plan for Fall Gelb also recognised the need for the swift neutralisation of Holland. The number of waterways meant that bridges could be blown and flood defences opened as an effective means of delaying a military advance into the country. In addition, von Bock, the Army Group B commander, thought a British force might be put ashore at Antwerp to reinforce the Dutch Army. To prevent all these possibilities it was decided to use 7. Flieger-Division to spearhead the invasion. The division would seize key bridges at Dordrecht, Rotterdam, Moerdijk, and over the Diep River. In addition it would land and secure

Left: Hitler inspecting the troops that took Eben Emael, one of a series of photographs of this event.

the main airfields in the west of Holland so that 22nd Air Landing Division could be brought in to take The Hague (and thereby the seat of government) and the approaches to Rotterdam.

All of 7. Flieger was involved. 1st and 2nd Battalions of 1st Parachute Regiment (I. and II./FJR 1) were to land on the Dordrecht and Moerdijk bridges. 3rd Battalion (III./FJR 1) was to land at Waalhaven, and six companies of 2nd Parachute Regiment (FJR 2) were to take Valkenburg and two smaller airfields nearby, backed up by 47th Infantry Regiment of 22nd Air Landing Division which would be air-landed quickly behind them.

These units moved to Münster, Paderborn, and Dortmund airports ready for the jump on Holland which was timed to take place 30 minutes after the jumps in Belgium. The first drop was III./FJR 1 (Hauptmann Schulz) at Waalhaven. This

Below: Hitler meeting Oberleutnant Meissner and Hauptmann Witzig at the award ceremony for the Eben Emael and Albert Canal missions.

Right: Hitler posing with the assault leaders of the raid on Eben Emael. Major Koch (promoted for his part in the mission) is to Hitler's right, Witzig next to Koch; to Hitler's left is Oberleutnant Meissner.

airfield was well defended by AA and ground troops but was quickly captured by the paratroops after a determined fight to take the control tower. They also took out an AA position that failed to surrender. Two regiments of 22nd Air Landing Division (Generalmajor Graf von Sponeck), 16th and 25th Infantry Regiments, came in as scheduled with the second wave, as did Generalleutnant Student and staff who set up 7. Flieger-Division HQ on the airfield.

II./FJR 1 (Hauptmann Prager) jumped north and south of the two long bridges (road and rail) over the Maas at Moerdijk and secured them safely even though the Dutch already had them wired for demolition. Leutnant Tietjen played a key part in storming the road bridge defences and its concrete pillboxes and was awarded the Knight's Cross for this. Actually II./FJR 1 had to hold these bridges for four days, much longer than anticipated, against sturdy Dutch assaults, including attacks by the crack Dutch Light Division which was falling back from the east. On 14 May the German perimeter round the bridges had still not been relieved. Student got together two paratroop companies from Waalhaven, together with the divisional artillery support (infantry gun and anti-tank gun companies) which had flown in with the second wave, and lorried them to the bridges where they engaged the Dutch attackers and gave much needed support until the SS *Leibstandarte Adolf Hitler* Regiment arrived, much delayed, to take over the positions.

The Dordrecht bridge was secured by I./FJR 1 (Hauptmann Walther), though the 3. Kompanie commander, Leutnant von Brandis, who had led the assault at Sola in Norway, was killed. The bridge was held for two days, again longer than had been anticipated, until the leading units of Eighteenth Army arrived. The paratroops suffered relatively heavy casualties.

The attack at Valkenburg was the least successful part of the whole operation. The drop by companies of FJR 2 on the airfield went according to plan, but the incoming Ju 52s found the ground too soft and sank into it on landing. Immobilised, they were an easy target for the defenders and many of the 47th Infantry's men were killed. Following aircraft had to be diverted, but the two small airfields nearby, Ypenburg and Ockenburg, had not been secured as the companies designated to take them had been wrongly positioned. One company landed at the Hook of Holland by mistake and had to make its way back, and many of the containers were lost or scattered. Ju 52s landing on these small unsecured airfields therefore ran into heavy defensive fire and 17 were destroyed, blocking these also. Remaining aircraft landed where they could, some on beaches near The Hague and ten on the main Hague–Rotterdam road, but even some of these veered off the road in cross-winds and were damaged. The final wave of aircraft was diverted to Waalhaven, the only safely held place to land.

The result of all this was heavy casualties and scrappy and confused fighting by the surviving paratroops and men of 22nd Division. The prime object of 47th Infantry Regiment had been to seize The Hague, and with it the Dutch government, high command, and royal family. None of this was achieved and the royal family and senior military staff were able to escape to England to continue the war in exile. Kesselring blamed Student for this fiasco, since he had landed with his troops too early, and at Waalhaven he was cut off from news of Valkenburg. However, in the general euphoria of victory, and the perceived success of the parachute operations, Student's reputation did not suffer.

Surrender in Holland came on 14 May, only four days after the invasion. It culminated in a savage bombing attack on Rotterdam which, owing to faulty communications, proceeded after Dutch surrender talks had already started. General Schmidt of XLIX Corps, who had become the area commander, ordered Generalleutnant Student to drive into Rotterdam and take charge of the surrender talks on the German side. Dutch and German troops were still clashing in the area. Hearing shooting outside the building where negotiations were taking place, Student went to the window to see what was happening. A stray German bullet hit him in the right forehead just behind his eye. His sight and life were saved by a skilled Dutch surgeon in a nearby hospital but he was hospitalised in Berlin until

Below: Men of Assault Group Koch, in full combat dress. The NCO on the left wears an Army eagle on his smock, but a Luftwaffe tunic and collar patches. This was not unusual in 1940 since a number of the troops involved were former members of the Army Fallschirm-Infanterie-Bataillon. Photo taken shortly after the unit had been relieved.

August 1940, and convalescent until January 1941. His speech was affected, but he did not lose his energy, determination or mental ability.

In Student's absence Generalmajor Richard Putzier took temporary command of 7. Flieger-Division. Because of the overall success of the invasion in the West, and the propaganda impact of the parachute landings, many of the shortcomings and limitations of the operation were overlooked, Hitler gave a well publicised reception to the men who captured Eben Emael and presented their bravery awards personally. Plans were approved to enlarge the airborne forces and open a second parachute training school. Göring basked in the publicity and praise his Luftwaffe paratroops received, and feted Student's leadership.

In reality losses had been high. Thanks mainly to the errors at Valkenburg some 40% of the officers and 28% of the men of 22nd Air Landing Division had been killed. Some of the parachute drops had also sustained high casualty rates and, of 430 Ju 52s in use, about 65% were destroyed or damaged beyond repair. The units engaged in the Valkenburg landings lost 90% of their aircraft. These high losses might well have limited airborne operations in the near future, had any been planned to take place.

OPERATION SEA LION

Though Operation Sea Lion (Seelöwe), the German invasion of Britain, was never to happen, it was planned in some considerable detail and, indeed, was altered in some aspects as time went by, particularly in respect of the proposed use of airborne troops.

The speed of the German campaign in the West surprised even the German high command and there was no immediate prospect of an invasion immediately following the Dunkirk withdrawal and the fall of France in June 1940. Not only would the forces need to be reorganised for an invasion, but it was necessary to have air superiority over the Channel and southern England (leading to the Battle of Britain in summer 1940) to keep the Royal Navy at bay, and time was required to assemble a large invasion fleet of barges to carry men, tanks and equipment across the Channel.

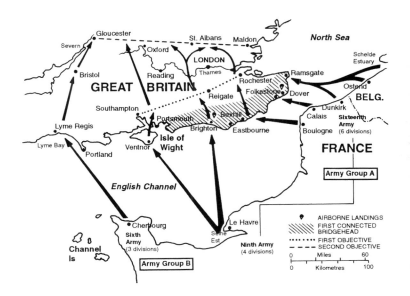

Operation Sea Lion—the projected invasion of Great Britain.

Clearly, with the perceived success of airborne forces in Belgium and Holland, they would also have a key role to play in an invasion of Britain. The impact and imagery of the May operations made German paratroops a powerful propaganda tool and there was a genuine 'parachute scare' in Britain through the rest of 1940, with German paratroops expected daily. German paratroops dropping disguised as nuns started as a serious rumour – one of many – before ending up as a joke. One of the major duties of the newly raised Home Guard (or LDV as it was first officially known) was to defend against parachute landings and one of the early nicknames for them was 'Parashots'.

To prevent glider and Ju 52 landings all flat fields and parklands were strewn with posts or old cars, and straight wide roads were provided with obstructions or bars which could be put in place quickly to prevent aircraft landings. Road signposts and even station names were removed to confuse the expected invaders, and church bells were banned, only to be rung as a warning in the event of air or sea invasion.

One result of the successful Eben Emael operation was a decision to expand Assault Group *Koch* into a full strength assault regiment (Fallschirmjäger-Sturmregiment) under command of Oberst Meindl, specifically for deployment in the proposed invasion. At one stage in the planning the new regiment was to land on the Dover coast-gun batteries and immobilise them in similar style to the guns of Eben Emael. Hitler, at first, had no fixed ideas about the deployment of the airborne forces and in his initial directive on 16 July 1940 he merely asked for suggestions, or whether they should be used as a mobile reserve. The first scheme put forward, however, was that paratroops would be dropped at Brighton and on the hills inland behind Dover to guard the west and east flanks of the sea landing, but 7. Flieger's acting commander, Putzier, was unhappy with this. Potential drop zones in these areas were well obstructed by the British and the lightly armed airborne troops would be very vulnerable to counter-attacks.

On 12 September the plans were changed, under the influence of Kesselring, and it was now proposed to take out the coastal gun batteries at Dover, as noted above, and land also north-west of Folkestone to secure the canal crossing at Hythe. Alternatives considered were dropping paratroops along the line Dymchurch–Bonnington–Kingsnorth–Woodchurch–New Romney to secure the Military Canal, and making another landing at Canterbury to cut off the great Stour sector. It was also proposed to land on Lympne airfield to secure it and fly in 22nd Air Landing Division in a copy of the Waalhaven/Valkenburg landings in Holland.

The most finalised plan along these lines went into great detail with the following deployments:

1. Kampfgruppe *Meindl* to land at Hythe, secure the Military Canal crossings and move along the line from Hythe rail station to Saltwood to prevent any outflanking moves by the British.

Above: German parachute troops jumping over Holland. 10 May 1940.

Above: Fallschirmjäger and Army infantry link up outside Rotterdam, May 1940, they are wearing full combat dress.

Right: A Fallschirmjäger during the 1940 advance on the west.

Opposite, Above: Crashed German Ju 52 transport, one of many that were lost in the invasion of Holland.

Opposite, Below: Fallschirmjäger dropping over Northern France, training jump, 23 November 1940.

Above: German parachute troops jumping over Holland, 10 May 1940.

2. Kampfgruppe *Stentzler* to drop and seize the heights at Paddlesworth and hold off any counter-attacks.

These two groups would be timed to drop as the landing craft carrying 17th Infantry Division hit the beach near Folkestone.

3. Kampfgruppe *Bräuer* to drop one hour later south of Postling. This enlarged group would consist of a complete parachute battalion, a parachute engineer battalion, the anti-tank company of FJR 1, all of FJR 2 and FJR 3, and an extra battalion as divisional reserve.

Once landed Kampfgruppe *Bräuer* was to take *Stentzler* under command and the combined force was to take Sandgate and the high ground west of Paddlesworth. FJR 2 was to move north of Postling and guard against attack from the north while FJR 3 was to secure the western flank with one battalion detached to capture and hold Lympe airfield for a later fly-in by 22nd Air Landing Division, possibly as late as S plus 5.

Because of the postponements and eventual cancellation of Operation Sea Lion all this became academic, but early in September 1940 the 7. Flieger-Division staff got as far as selecting the airfields in France and Flanders that would used as departure points, and organising the logistics for getting the units into place, and the Kampfgruppen (assault groups) were set up as outlined in the plans. Student, still on sick leave, took an outside interest in all this and was personally opposed to concentrating the bulk of the airborne forces in the Folkestone area. He had other ideas, too, such as fitting Ju 52s with long range tanks so that 7. Flieger could later be used in the invasion of Northern Ireland. Hitler himself suggested parachute landings to seize Plymouth and Cornwall in later stages of the invasion, but by the time these matters were discussed in January 1941 the whole invasion idea was little more than fantasy.

OPERATION ATTILA

Another scheme which came to nothing was the plan to neutralise the French fleet at Toulon, should it attempt to leave harbour and defect to the Allied side. Under the terms of the Vichy Agreement, the fleet was supposed to remain inactive and southern France was not occupied, so any defection would take time to rectify. Hitler asked Student, in December 1940, for a contingency plan should the French fleet start to leave port. Student's first task on returning to duty on 1 January 1941, was to work this out. After sending a staff officer in disguise to visit the port area, and studying reconnaissance photographs, Student suggested that while the fleet was still raising steam, 7. Flieger assault troops would land by glider on the adjacent jetties alongside the ships in Eben Emael style, while a parachute drop secured the rest of the port area. He suggested that some naval men fly in with the gliders to deal with scuttling attempts and close down engine rooms, etc. Some naval personnel were selected for this. The project was named Operation Attila but the need to activate it never arose.

XI. FLIEGERKORPS IS FORMED

While Student was recuperating in the autumn of 1940, the decision was taken by OKH to increase the German airborne forces from divisional to corps strength. Student was promoted to General der Flieger and became corps commander. He took most of his 7. Flieger-Division staff with him, so Student's successor as divisional commander, Generalleutnant Süssmann, had to appoint a new staff. The corps was vested as XI. Fliegerkorps in January 1941. The chief of staff was Generalmajor Schlemm and the chief operations officer (1a) was Oberstleutnant Trettner.

XI. Fliegerkorps initially comprised Corps HQ, 7. Flieger-Division, 22nd Air Landing Division, plus the newly expanded Fallschirmjäger-Sturmregiment (Oberst Meindl) as corps troops, along with a flak battalion, a medical Abteilung, the parachute training schools, and various small transport and logistic units.

THE CORINTH CANAL

Bulgaria had intended to remain a neutral state but events in the Balkans in 1940/early 1941, including the Italian invasion of Greece, made Hitler decide to

Below: Men of FJR 2 drop to link up with the force at the bridge over the Corinth Canal.

bring Bulgaria under the Axis sphere of influence. Following heavy pressure, the Bulgarian prime minister signed a co-operation pact with the Axis on 1 March 1941, and German forces moved in at once. OKW considered that airborne forces would be useful in expelling the British from Greece and the Aegean islands in the offensive called Operation Marita which was to start on 6 April 1941. British troops from Libya and Egypt had been sent to aid the Greeks when Italy launched its flagging invasion of that country.

Early in March 1941 a brigade group, essentially a strengthened 2nd Parachute Regiment (FJR 2) under command of Generalleutnant Süssmann was sent to Plovdiv in Bulgaria. The initial intention was for it to drop on the island of Lemnos which commanded the entrance to the Dardanelles and was strategically important for possible future air operations, against the Romanian oil fields for example. But Lemnos was only lightly defended by the British, as it turned out, and it fell at once to a small German force landing by boat, so the paratroops were not required.

The Greek campaign was fast moving once Operation Marita started. The Yugoslav Army surrendered on 17 April, forcing the British under General Wilson to withdraw quickly south. Then Greek forces in Epirus were cut off and forced to surrender on 23 April, and complete withdrawal of British troops to Crete and Egypt was considered essential to avoid a similar fate. Greek harbours were now under Luftwaffe air attack and the small ports of the Peloponnese had to be used. The only route there was the bridge over the Corinth Canal and, if this could be taken, the British would be severely disrupted and certainly curtailed in their plans.

FJR 2 was moved to Larissa in Greece for the attack on the morning of 26 April, having under command I. and II./FJR 2 plus an assault engineer company, a signal company, a medical company, and an artillery company. The assault engineers were to land by the bridge in gliders at 07.00, seize it, and remove any demolition devices. The rest were to drop by parachute each side of the bridge to form a bridgehead. It was considered a hazardous mission, not least because of the stream of British troops crossing the bridge and moving south. But the surprise factor was thought to outweigh this. The glider landing was made by 6. Kompanie of II./FJR 2 (Leutnant Hans Teusen) and went to plan. But the bridge was blown just as the assault engineers removed the charges, the explosion being caused it is thought by either a stray British AA shell hitting the explosives or canny British troops firing at them. Some of the assault engineers were killed as the bridge went down. By now the Ju 52s carrying the paratroops had arrived overhead and dropped I. Bataillon to the north and II. Bataillon to the south of the bridge. Despite the mayhem of the explosion, and much British small arms fire, casualties were few but one Ju 52 flew into the mountain side killing all but two aboard, and some paratroops landed in the deeply gorged canal and were drowned.

Teusen's men moved south after the withdrawing British troops. They took the Corinth airfield and next day moved on, taking the surrender of about 900 British and 1,500 Greek troops after Teusen made out they were part of a much larger German invasion force. For this enterprise, Teusen was awarded the Knight's Cross. I. Bataillon to the north held out in the bridgehead for two days until German ground troops arrived on 28 April. By then the assault engineers had built a new temporary bridge over the canal. One feature of the operation which aided the paratroops was a plentiful supply of British Army vehicles which were captured and used to give much needed mobility.

While the Corinth Canal operation was successful as far as it went, it would have been much more useful had it been staged two days earlier, for then virtually all the British troops would have been bottled up on the Greek mainland and might

Left: Maps showing the Crete operation. The top one shows the landings of 20 May; the bottom the battle in the north of the island.

Below: Fallschirmjäger jumping over Crete during the second-wave landings on Heraklion during the afternoon of 20 May 1941.

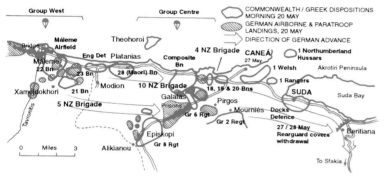

never have been able to withdraw to Crete or Egypt. Student was very displeased since the operation was mounted at very short notice with no reference to, or consultation with, XI. Fliegerkorps HQ in Berlin, even though it had been sanctioned by Hitler. By this time planning was under way for the much more ambitious Operation Mercury (*Merkur*) to capture Crete and in Student's view the use of paratroops at Corinth compromised security in the Aegean area by prematurely revealing the presence of the airborne forces which would be so vital in that battle.

CRETE

Student considered the taking of Crete to be a logical conclusion to the Operation Marita campaign. It could have several advantages. First it would remove the British forces from the Aegean area and prevent it being used by them as an air base for bombing the Ploesti oil-fields in Romania. Then it could provide a useful staging post for further airborne operations against the Suez Canal, Cyprus, Malta, or even Syria. He put his ideas to Hitler, via the good offices of Göring, on 20 April 1941.

Hitler was dismissive of the further objectives like Suez and Malta, but he approved of the idea of taking Crete itself. Hitler appreciated the idea of having the island in German hands to remove the chances of it being used as an air base by the British, but he also saw it as a good diversion from Operation Barbarossa, the invasion of Russia due to begin in early summer and in the advanced planning stage. His approval for what was designated Operation Mercury came in a directive of 25 April with the proviso that it should be carried out as soon as possible, and should not conflict with the launch of Barbarossa. Some units, such as the air component, might be needed for Barbarossa afterwards.

Below: Pioneer with a standard light flamethrower in action on Crete.

The soonest possible date was 17 May which left just over three weeks for planning and positioning of the troops, a very tight schedule indeed. In the pace of developments both sides suffered from either making the wrong assumptions or faulty interpretation of intelligence. Student correctly assumed the Luftwaffe would have air superiority, for he could count on fighter cover and dive bombers from the nearby Greek bases, and the transports and gliders, too, had only a short hop from Greece. The RAF had only a few fighters on Crete, and there were just a few old tanks and small numbers of field and AA guns, too, for Crete had been low priority in defence terms, garrisoned by just three battalions to defend the naval base at Suda Bay. Student assumed that the bulk of the British and Commonwealth forces evacuated from Greece had been taken to Egypt, leaving only token numbers in Crete, but many men had, in fact, moved only as far as Crete and there were over 25,000 men there.

Ultra intercepts gave the British an awareness that something was planned in the Aegean area, but the exact nature of what was intended was not clear at first. It was known in April that Ju 52s of XI. Fliegerkorps had moved to the Balkans and that 22. Luftlande-Division (Air Landing

Division) was to move to Yugoslavia. Also that General Süssmann of 7. Flieger-Division was in the area receiving signals. But this did not necessarily point to Crete, as the Corinth Canal landing (Operation Hannibal to the Germans) showed on 26 April. However, intensive air reconnaissance sorties took place over Crete on 24–25 April, and signals were intercepted concerning extra aviation supplies and orders not to bomb airfields on Crete or mine Suda Bay. Crete was clearly high on the list for invasion and General Wavell, C-in-C Middle East, ordered the tough dynamic New Zealander General Bernard Freyberg to the island on 30 April to organise the defence. Though depleted, and short of equipment due to losses in Greece, there were three infantry brigades, New Zealand, Australian, and British, which Freyberg deployed west, centre, and east of the island respectively.

On 6 May Ultra intercepted an important signal which gave virtually the entire schedule and order of battle for the forthcoming Crete invasion, complete with all landing areas and objectives. It also revealed there would be a follow-up of more troops, equipment, and supplies brought in by sea, all to be ready for 17 May. This was one of the most complete revelations of plans that Ultra came up with in the whole war and Freyberg was one of the first recipients of intelligence on this scale. In the circumstances he made the best possible use of it by having his men ready and waiting at all the drop zones and objectives and able to give the paratroops a hard fight. Intercepts picked up that the operation was delayed, largely due to late arrival of aviation fuel, first to 18 May then to 20 May. The defenders over-estimated the importance of the sea landings and slightly under-estimated the strength of the air landings, particularly at Maleme, but overall the valuable knowledge was exploited to the full. The biggest surprise for the Germans was finding how well the British and Commonwealth forces were disposed to meet them, for they were of course unaware that Ultra had intercepted their plans.

For the landing on Crete, XI. Fliegerkorps was greatly augmented. The original Fallschirmjäger-Sturmregiment had been re-designated as the Luftlande-Sturmregiment (air landing assault regiment – LLStR) with four battalions as part

Above: Fallschirmjäger in action on Crete during the tough fighting that followed the landings.

Above: Ramcke handing out medals to survivors of the Crete operation, summer 1941.

of the corps troops. It was virtually a small division in its own right, reflected in the promotion of its commander, Meindl, to Generalmajor. 7. Flieger had three three-battalion regiments and strong divisional troops including a machine-gun, anti-tank, and pioneer battalions and artillery batteries. The 5. Gebirgs Division (5. Gebirgs-Division – Generalmajor Ringel) had replaced the 22nd Division as air landing division, partly to save moving the 22nd Division which had been moved to Romania to protect the oil-fields, and partly because a mountain division was thought more suited to the rugged Crete terrain. Student had initial misgivings about this change, partly because he did not get on with Ringel, but also because the division had no previous air landing experience. However, 5. Gebirgs Division was considered a crack unit and certainly proved invaluable in Crete.

The logistical problems of getting all the units and equipment to Greece were considerable. The gliders, for example, had to be shipped in components by rail, sheeted over for security, and all air and rail movements had to be dovetailed into the movements readying forces for Barbarossa which would begin soon, and Barbarossa movements had priority. The logistical task was so complex it had its own code name, Operation Flying Dutchman.

There proved to be a shortage of Ju 52s which meant the landing had to be made in two waves with the same aircraft used twice. There were four landing zones to be attacked by three groups. Group West was to take and secure the important Maleme airfield. Group Centre was to take the island capital Canea, Suda Bay and Retimo airfield. Group East was to take the town and airfield of Heraklion. The first wave was to go in early in the morning to take Maleme, Canea and Suda Bay, and the same aircraft would return at 13.00 with the second wave to take Retimo and Heraklion airfields.

VIII. Fliegerkorps aircraft had started attacking targets in Crete on 14 May, concentrating on the AA defences of the airfields and Suda Bay. Just before the landing on 20 May, VIII. Fliegerkorps carried out intensive bombing of defence positions to the west of the island. As the bombing run ended, I./LLStR landed in gliders to take Maleme airfield and AA positions near Canea and Suda Bay. One mission was to secure the bridge over the Tavronitis River. The other LLStR battalions dropped west and east of Maleme. II./LLStR (Major Stentzler) was charged with taking Hill 107, the high ground dominating Maleme airfield, but this took until next day due to stubborn resistance by 22nd New Zealand Battalion which even withstood Stuka attacks on its positions. FJR 3 parachuted on to the plain southwest of Canea.

III./LLStR took particularly heavy casualties when the men jumped. They were widely scattered, as were their containers, and so many were killed or wounded that the unit was no longer battle-worthy. II./FJR 3 suffered a similar fate. LLStR's commander, Meindl, was among the early casualties and Major Stentzler of II./LLStR took over command. 7. Flieger's commander, Generalleutnant Süssmann died when his glider crashed on landing.

The first-wave landings, in short, were a failure with only minor objectives taken, and too many men landing in the wrong place. The second wave fared even worse. It was delayed by late returning aircraft, slow refuelling by hand from jerricans, and huge dust clouds which slowed the take-off rate. Thus the second-wave drops were late and staggered and were no longer synchronised with the scheduled bombing runs which preceded them. FJR 2 dropped at Retimo but was pinned down by the defenders and failed to take the airfield. FJR 1 and II./FJR 2 landed at Heraklion but took heavy casualties as they jumped, had two companies decimated, and were scattered so widely it took all night to round up the survivors. They failed to take the airfield as intended.

The first day of operations had been close to disastrous, though little of this was known until evening by General Student back at HQ in Greece. Fortunately for the Germans there were only a few minor unco-ordinated Allied counter-attacks during the night, for a really concentrated counter-attack could well have wiped them out. The plans called for 5. Gebirgs Division to land on Retimo and Heraklion airfield on 21 May, but as there was no certainty these would be secured in time, concentration was switched to Maleme where there was at least a foothold. Even so Maleme airfield was not finally taken until 14.00 on 21 May after more Stuka attacks and the dropping of the two last LLStR companies. Student now sent in Oberst Ramcke, one of his staff officers who had been teaching 5. Gebirgs Division air landing skills, to take over command from the injured Meindl. Ramcke dropped at Maleme soon after it was secured, bringing with him a reserve battalion to make up the numbers after the heavy casualties. At 15.00 the first Ju 52s landed bringing in the mountain troops, a welcome sight to the hard pressed paratroops. Congestion on the small airfield as Ju 52s crowded in caused a few collisions and wrecks, however.

The sea landings, in two convoys largely composed of commandeered Greek caiques, were also disastrous. Two mountain division battalions, some 7. Flieger divisional troops, guns and supplies, were almost all lost when both convoys were virtually wiped out by powerful Royal Navy forces, though this was at some expense to the Royal Navy who lost two destroyers (one of them the famous *Kelly*) and a cruiser to Luftwaffe air attack. Prospects still looked bleak for the invaders.

A counter-attack at Maleme airfield was beaten back on the night of 21–22 May and Student and the divisional HQ flew in on the evening of 22 May. By this time three battalions of 5. Gebirgs Division were in place. That evening General Ringel took command of the western part of the island and moved his men south-east into the mountains to turn the New Zealand flank just west of Canea. The

Below: All the drops over Crete were made at low level. Here the technique is practised at a training school.

Above: DFS 230 glider of I./LLStR alongside Tavronitis Bridge, between Maleme and Suda Bay, one of the objectives successfully captured by the Fallschirmjäger.

Left: This Ju 52 has been hit by anti-aircraft fire and is about to fall from the sky. Only five paras have got out so far.

Opposite, Above: II./LLStR after taking the vital Hill 107 on 21 May. The flag is to show attacking aircraft that the location is in German hands.

Opposite, Below: Matilda knocked out by II./FJR 1 near Heraklion airfield.

Above: Paras drop over Crete. This action convinced the Allies there was a future for airborne troops; it convinced Hitler that airborne operations were too costly in manpower and munitions.

Opposite, Above: Men of 7. FJD in action in Russia during the late autumn of 1941.

Opposite, Below: MG 42 team in winter camouflage in Russia.

reorganised survivors of the Luftlande-Sturmregiment, now commanded by Ramcke, plus 100. Gebirgs Regiment, made a frontal attack near the coast road and captured Canea on 26–27 May. Ringel's men pushed on east to relieve the paratroops still stuck at Retimo and Heraklion, and Freyberg decided to evacuate his troops from the island on 27 May, ordering all remaining British and Commonwealth troops south to Sfakia where Royal Navy ships took them off. 100. Gebirgs Regiment (Oberst Utz) had a good campaign. They set off in hot pursuit of the retreating troops and captured 10,000 of them, leaving only 17,000 to be evacuated. The last of them had gone by 31 May and Crete was now wholly in German hands after a very short but bloody campaign. Freyberg's withdrawal was largely due to lack of equipment and reinforcements, not due to lack of courage, intelligence or fighting qualities. He was short of radios, guns and tanks for so much had been lost in Greece, and the lack of resources at Middle East Command meant he was left to do the best he could with the under-equipped forces available. Air support was virtually non-existent.

British and Commonwealth casualties were about 2,500 dead and wounded and over 10,000 captured, and 2,011 naval men were lost in the sea actions. In XI. Fliegerkorps, losses were 3,352 dead and missing, and 3,400 wounded out of a force of 22,000. The XI. Fliegerkorps' men moved back to Germany in mid-July 1941 when relieved by occupation troops. The losses and carnage of the Crete campaign had a deep effect on Hitler and the high command. Essentially it saw the end of full scale airborne operations by the Luftwaffe. At a gallantry awards ceremony for men of the campaign on 19 August 1941, Hitler said to Student: 'Crete has shown that the days of paratroopers are finished. The parachute force is purely and simply a weapon of surprise. The factor of surprise has now been used up.'

Crete was, indeed, the last set-piece airborne operation by the Germans. They were costly in fuel, aircraft, resources, and men. From mid-1941 onwards the paratroops fought mainly as elite ground troops, though there were a few occasions when small airborne operations were mounted.

THE RUSSIAN FRONT

From June 1941 most German high command concentration was on Operation Barbarossa, the invasion of Russia. In that month there was a small scale air drop when paratroopers were used to seize intact bridges over the River Dvina to let the Brandenburg Division pass through. In September 1941 II./LLStR was sent by air direct from its base at Goslar to attack a Russian bridgehead over the Neva near Petruschino on the Leningrad front. Though they succeeded in pushing back the Russians, they suffered heavy casualties including the death of the commander, Major Stentzler. Later that month FJR 1, FJR 3, and 7. Flieger-Division HQ and divisional troops also went to the Leningrad front, now under command of Generalmajor Petersen. By 17 November, 7. Flieger had repulsed 146 Russian attacks in 46 days, destroyed 41 Soviet tanks and taken 3,400 prisoners, though sustaining over 3,000 killed or wounded itself. The commander of Sixteenth Army paid a special tribute to the division's fine fighting record over this period.

FJR 2 was sent to Mius in winter 1941–42 and saw hard fighting as part of the resistance to the attempted breakout from Leningrad. I./LLStR (Major Koch) was used to defend the key Anisowo-Gorodishche airfield near Moscow in winter 1941–42, repulsing heavy attacks, while sometimes cut off, in severe winter weather.

XI. FLIEGERKORPS AS AT 20 MAY 1941 (THE BATTLE OF CRETE)

XI. FLIEGERKORPS HQ

CO General der Flieger Student
Chief of Staff Generalmajor Schlemm
Ia Oberstleutnant i.G. Trettner
QM Oberstleutnant Seibt
Ic Hauptmann Mors
IW (weather) Regierungsrat Dr Brand
IIa Oberst v. Fichte
IIb Oberstleutnant Ehrlich
Signals officer Oberstleutnant Dr Weyland
Engineer staff officer Oberstleutnant Barenthin
Weapons and equipment Major Käthler
IVa Oberregierungsrat Hopf
IVb Oberfeldarzt Dr Höfer
Field reporting Kriegsgerichtsrat Rüdel

XI. FLIEGERKORPS TROOPS

Corps Reconnaissance Flight

Transport Flight XI

Transport Company

Ln Section 41 (mot)

Fallschirm lt AA Battalion

Fallschirm Medical Section

Luftlande-Sturm (Assault)-Regiment

HQ (CO Generalmajor Meindl)

I Battalion (CO Major Koch)
II Battalion (CO Major Stentzler)
III Battalion (CO Major Scherber)
IV Battalion (CO Hauptmann Gericke)

7. FLIEGER-DIVISION

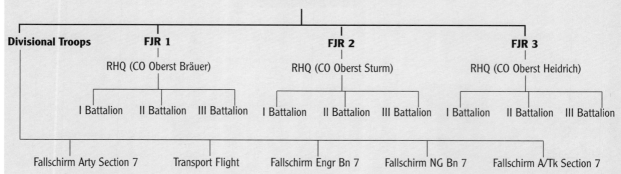

Division HQ
Generalleutnant Süssmann

Divisional Troops

FJR 1
RHQ (CO Oberst Bräuer)
I Battalion   II Battalion   III Battalion

FJR 2
RHQ (CO Oberst Sturm)
I Battalion   II Battalion   III Battalion

FJR 3
RHQ (CO Oberst Heidrich)
I Battalion   II Battalion   III Battalion

Fallschirm Arty Section 7   Transport Flight   Fallschirm Engr Bn 7   Fallschirm NG Bn 7   Fallschirm A/Tk Section 7

5. GEBIRGS-DIVISION

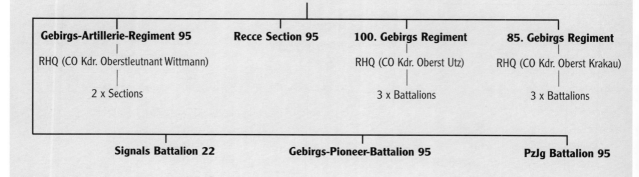

Division HQ
Generalmajor Ringel

Gebirgs-Artillerie-Regiment 95
RHQ (CO Kdr. Oberstleutnant Wittmann)
2 x Sections

Recce Section 95

100. Gebirgs Regiment
RHQ (CO Kdr. Oberst Utz)
3 x Battalions

85. Gebirgs Regiment
RHQ (CO Kdr. Oberst Krakau)
3 x Battalions

Signals Battalion 22   **Gebirgs-Pioneer-Battalion 95**   **PzJg Battalion 95**

1. FALLSCHIRMJÄGER DIVISION AT THE SECOND BATTLE OF CASSINO

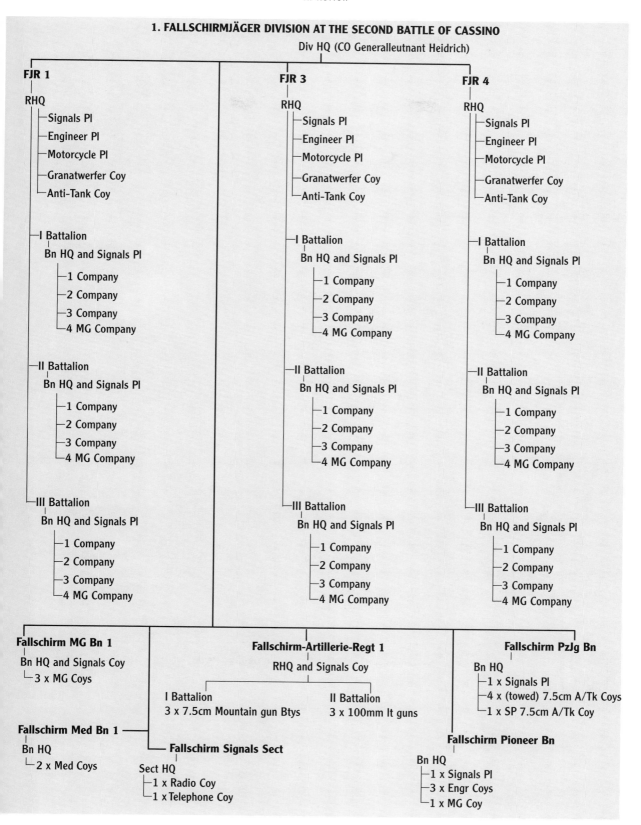

Div HQ (CO Generalleutnant Heidrich)

FJR 1

RHQ
- Signals Pl
- Engineer Pl
- Motorcycle Pl
- Granatwerfer Coy
- Anti-Tank Coy

I Battalion
Bn HQ and Signals Pl
- 1 Company
- 2 Company
- 3 Company
- 4 MG Company

II Battalion
Bn HQ and Signals Pl
- 1 Company
- 2 Company
- 3 Company
- 4 MG Company

III Battalion
Bn HQ and Signals Pl
- 1 Company
- 2 Company
- 3 Company
- 4 MG Company

FJR 3

RHQ
- Signals Pl
- Engineer Pl
- Motorcycle Pl
- Granatwerfer Coy
- Anti-Tank Coy

I Battalion
Bn HQ and Signals Pl
- 1 Company
- 2 Company
- 3 Company
- 4 MG Company

II Battalion
Bn HQ and Signals Pl
- 1 Company
- 2 Company
- 3 Company
- 4 MG Company

III Battalion
Bn HQ and Signals Pl
- 1 Company
- 2 Company
- 3 Company
- 4 MG Company

FJR 4

RHQ
- Signals Pl
- Engineer Pl
- Motorcycle Pl
- Granatwerfer Coy
- Anti-Tank Coy

I Battalion
Bn HQ and Signals Pl
- 1 Company
- 2 Company
- 3 Company
- 4 MG Company

II Battalion
Bn HQ and Signals Pl
- 1 Company
- 2 Company
- 3 Company
- 4 MG Company

III Battalion
Bn HQ and Signals Pl
- 1 Company
- 2 Company
- 3 Company
- 4 MG Company

Fallschirm MG Bn 1
Bn HQ and Signals Coy
- 3 x MG Coys

Fallschirm Med Bn 1
Bn HQ
- 2 x Med Coys

Fallschirm-Artillerie-Regt 1
RHQ and Signals Coy

I Battalion
3 x 7.5cm Mountain gun Btys

II Battalion
3 x 100mm lt guns

Fallschirm Signals Sect
Sect HQ
- 1 x Radio Coy
- 1 x Telephone Coy

Fallschirm PzJg Bn
Bn HQ
- 1 x Signals Pl
- 4 x (towed) 7.5cm A/Tk Coys
- 1 x SP 7.5cm A/Tk Coy

Fallschirm Pioneer Bn
Bn HQ
- 1 x Signals Pl
- 3 x Engr Coys
- 1 x MG Coy

Right: Unusual provisions—airdropping a goat as food for paras on Crete.

Below : Tunisia, 1942. BMW RI2 and sidecar (or other equivalent motorcycles) were the largest vehicles airdropped or carried in the Ju 52. They were used to tow light guns and trailers and by recce units.

In late summer 1942, Hitler suggested a parachute operation to take the key passes in the Caucasus for a mountain division offensive, but this was cancelled after further study showed it to be of doubtful tactical value, so 7. Flieger-Division moved out of Russia, first to France, then back to Germany. However, in October 1942 the division was sent to Smolensk to hold a 90km (56-mile) front extending north to Velizh. This proved a quiet front, however, and FJR 1 was used temporarily to reinforce the defence of Orel while FJR 3 took part in an attack to relieve a surrounded garrison at Velikiye Luki. In November 1942 7. Flieger-Division was renamed 1. Fallschirmjäger Division (1. FJD), and was now commanded by Generalmajor Heidrich. A new 2. Fallschirmjäger Division (2. FJD) was also formed, commanded by Generalmajor Ramcke. In spring 1943 both divisions were sent to France as reserve forces, 1. FJD to Avignon and 2. FJD to Nîmes.

NORTH AFRICA

In spring 1942, British forces based on Malta were causing severe problems to the supply routes across the Mediterranean to sustain Rommel's *Afrika Korps*. Hitler and Mussolini agreed with Kesselring, now the Mediterranean Luftwaffe commander, that Malta should be taken in the summer of that year — Operation Hercules. This would involve a drop by 30,000 German and Italian paratroops, the latter being available because Generalmajor Ramcke had been heading a training mission in Italy to create the *Folgore* Parachute Division. Six Italian Army divisions would simultaneously invade by sea supported by the Italian Navy. Planning by Student's staff started in April 1942 with Ramcke designated as the airborne force commander. Planning was at an advanced stage when Hitler had second thoughts

Below: FJR 3 en route to Sicily to reinforce German troops after the Allied invasion, 12 July 1943.

Above: German Fallschirmjäger during the defence of Cassino, dug in after the aerial bombing.

Opposite, Above: Mussolini at Gran Sasso, 12 September 1943. Skorzeny is to his right. Note the Fallschirmjäger behind Mussolini is wearing a standard German helmet rather than a para one, an increasingly common occurrence towards the end of the war.

Opposite, Below: On of the DFS 230 gliders on the Italian, Gran Sasso, 12 September 1943.

and cancelled the operation, swayed by a low opinion of the Italian contribution on which success depended.

Ramcke's men, already assembling in Italy in brigade strength, were sent instead as an independent brigade group, Fallschirmjäger Brigade *Ramcke*, to reinforce Rommel's hard-pressed *Afrika Korps*. In August 1942 they arrived at Alamein. In the main battle at Alamein the brigade was forced into a fighting withdrawal on 2 November at the height of Eighth Army's onslaught. In the confusion the paratroops lost most of their transport and supplies, and communication, too, but on 6 November they ambushed a complete British armoured brigade supply column with all its stores and with this captured transport and booty they pulled back with relative ease until they caught up with the rest of the *Afrika Korps* west of Mersa Matruh. For this initiative Ramcke was awarded the Oak Leaves to his Iron Cross, and returned to Europe to give further distinguished service.

After Operation Torch, the North Africa landings, Tunisia was under threat and FJR 5, a newly raised regiment commanded by Major Koch, was sent out in December 1942, together with 21st Parachute Engineer Battalion (Major Witzig) Both commanders were veterans of Eben Emael. They had to cover a 500km (300-mile) front and took part in hard fighting including the offensive that took Bou Arada. The units stayed in Tunisia until the German forces there surrendered on 12 May 1943.

ITALY

When the Allies landed in Sicily on 10 July 1943 1. Fallschirmjäger Division was airlifted from its Avignon base to Rome, for onward transit to Sicily. FJR 3

(Oberstleutnant Heilmann) made a parachute jump into Catania, Sicily, on 12 July to secure the airport for the rest of the division to fly in. But the Allied bridgehead was already well established and the German forces could do little to stem the tide. With the Luftwaffe *Hermann Göring* Panzer-Division 1. FJD made a fighting withdrawal to Messina from where German forces were being evacuated. 1. FJD acted as a rearguard and was the last to leave on 17 August. In one notable incident of the campaign, on 15 July, FJR 3 was cut off by British forces near Cantania but escaped to join the others by creeping away quietly in single file during the night under an unguarded bridge.

When Marshal Badoglio's government ousted Mussolini on 25 July Il Duce was taken to the island of Ponza, then on to La Maddalena in Sardinia. XI. Fliegerkorps under Student was now sent to Rome, taking also 2. FJD under command when it was flown in from its Nîmes base. 3. Panzergrenadier-Division was also taken under corps command. 2. FJD came from the north and 3. Panzergrenadier-Division from the south to secure Rome and keep open lines of communication to the south. The government and Italian royal family were forced to leave.

In Italy Eighth Army troops landed in Calabria on 3 September, and FJR 3 was in action again. Italy surrendered and the new Badoglio government joined the Allies. The US Fifth Army landed at Salerno where FJR 4 and the *Hermann Göring* Division were the main defenders, the battle for the Salerno beachhead lasting until 17 September. All the regiments of 1. FJD now came together under divisional command and took part in the fighting withdrawal north.

Several parachute operations followed. When the Italian army surrendered, II./FJR 6 (formerly IV./LLStR, Major Gericke) flew from Foggia to drop on Monte Rotondo, near Rome, to capture the Italian Army chief, General Roatta. After fighting into his HQ they found he and his staff had already fled to Pescara. Next came the rescue of Mussolini, which was entrusted to SS-Hauptsturmführer Skorzeny who was assigned the Paratroop Demonstration Battalion under Major

Left: Cassino—Fallschirmjäger counter-attacking the New Zealanders.

Opposite, Above: Well-armed Fallschirmjäger—several carrying the FG42 parachute assault rifle which was being troop-tested at the time of the Gran-Sasso raid. It proved unsatisfactory but further development lead to the StuG 44, used in the last year of the war.

Opposite, Below: Anti-tank gunners man a 2.8cm PaK 41 near a roadblock in Rome (see caption on page 56). Both men wear helmet netting. An open ammunition box lies ready behind the gun. The gunlayer sports a field dressing on his right arm.

KORPS-FALLSCHIRM-PIONEER BATTALION, 1942

HQ

HQ Company

Signals Platoon

Battle Strength c716 all ranks

Firepower:

LMGs	36
MMGs	8
A/tk rifles	12
Small flamethrowers	12

4 x Companies

HQ

─3 x Platoons

Pl HQ
1 x small flamethrower
1 x A/tk rifle

─Section
─Section
─Section
Each 1 x LMG

─Med MG Section

Light Engineer Company

6 x large rubber boats
12 x small rubber boats

Notes:
(a) Organisation, strength and firepower provisional.
(b) It is not known whether there is any standard allotment of engineer stores to the battalion. Personnel are intensively trained in the use of mines and demolition stores of all types (including those used in assaults on fixed defences). Stores actually carried on an operation will be carefully selected in accordance with tactical requirements.

FALLSCHIRM-ARTILLERIE-ABTEILUNG, 1942-43

HQ ——— **HQ Company**

Signals Section
6 x W/T sub secs (?)
1 x Sig exchange (?) det

3 x Troops

HQ

─1 x Infantry Platoon
6 x Sections
Each 1 x LMG

─1 x Signals Section of:
4 x W/T sub sections
2 x telephone sub-sections

─ 1 x Gun Echelon of:
2 x Gun Sections
Each two 10.5cm lt recoilless guns

Battle Strength c461 all ranks

Firepower:

10.5cm lt recoilless guns	12
LMGs	18
A/tk rifles	6

Transport (airborne)

Motorcycles	4
Motorcycle combinations	18
Bicycles	6
Ammunition carts	24

Right: Paras in Holland, 1940. The MG34 team has recovered the weapon from its container and is readying it for action. By 1942–43 the Fallschirmjäger had become ground troops in all but name.

IX. FLIEGERKORPS, 1941–42

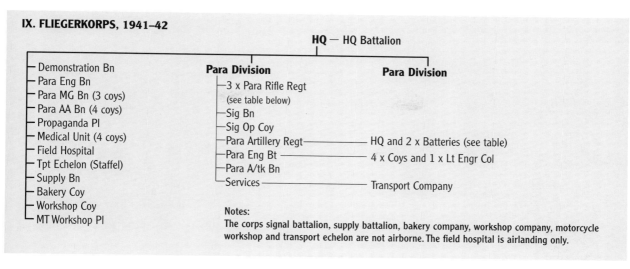

HQ — HQ Battalion

- Demonstration Bn
- Para Eng Bn
- Para MG Bn (3 coys)
- Para AA Bn (4 coys)
- Propaganda Pl
- Medical Unit (4 coys)
- Field Hospital
- Tpt Echelon (Staffel)
- Supply Bn
- Bakery Coy
- Workshop Coy
- MT Workshop Pl

Para Division
- 3 x Para Rifle Regt
  (see table below)
- Sig Bn
- Sig Op Coy
- Para Artillery Regt——————— HQ and 2 x Batteries (see table)
- Para Eng Bt ——————————— 4 x Coys and 1 x Lt Engr Col
- Para A/tk Bn
- Services ——————————————— Transport Company

Para Division

Notes:
The corps signal battalion, supply battalion, bakery company, workshop company, motorcycle
workshop and transport echelon are not airborne. The field hospital is airlanding only.

FALLSCHIRMJÄGER-REGIMENT, 1942-43

HQ — HQ Company, inc Sig Pl and Pioneer Pl

Infantry Gun Company
7.5cm mountain or light
recoilless guns

3 x Battalions
HQ

PzJg Company
2.8cm or 4.2cm A/Tk guns

- 3 x Lt Rifle Companies
  Each of:
  HQ, 3 x Rifle Platoons,
  Signals Platoon, A/Tk Sect
  (of 2 x 2.8cm guns)

- 1 x Hy Rifle Company of:
  HQ, 2 x Med MG Pl (2 Sects of
  2 MMGs), 1 x Rifle Pl, 1 Med Mor
  Sect (2 x 5cm mortars), 1 x A/Tk
  Sect (2 x 2.8cm guns)

Establishment strength c3,100 all ranks
Battle strength c2,200 all ranks
Firepower:

LMGs	198
MMGs	24
5cm mortars	30
8cm mortars	6
7.5cm mtn (or lt recoilless) guns	8
2.8cm A/Tk guns	33
(or 2.8cm x 24 and 4.2cm x 9)	

Notes:
Considerable variations in organization to suit the
tactical requirements. The following variations have
been noted in a para rifle regiment employed in
ground fighting:
(a) A/tk Sects in rifle coys equipped with A/Tk
rifles in place of 2.8cm guns. The A/Tk Coy was
apparently to be equipped with nine 5cm guns.
(b) The Inf Gun Coy was equipped with nine
10.5cm light recoilless guns, seven 15cm rocket
projectors and three A/Tk rifles.

Left: Para and motorcycle in Belgium. Solo and
sidecar combos were dropped with the troops and were
used for reconnaissance and transport.

Above: Units of 2. FJD were airlifted to the south of Rome in July 1943 to hold the city against a possible Italian coup. Here the unit attacks Italian forces commanded by General Carboni who were protecting Rome and the King's palace.

Opposite, Above: Flak Vierling in Normandy. The Quad version was only used in ground fighting since it could not be carried in a Junkers Ju 52.

Opposite, Below left: Generalleutnant Meindl, commander of II. Fallschirmkorps (3. FJD and 5. FJD) with Rommel, commander in chief Army Group B.

Opposite, Below right: Hermann Göring in early 1945 with Generalleutnant Schmalz, the commander of the eponymous 'Hermann Göring' Fallschirm-Pz-Korps.

Mors for the task. It was discovered that Mussolini had been secretly taken from La Maddalena to a mountain hotel on the Gran Sasso, Abruzzi. On 12 September a paratroop company landed by glider alongside the hotel, freed Mussolini, and flew him out in a Fieseler Storch which Hauptmann Gerlach had landed expertly in front of the hotel. They took him to Rome, then on to Rastenburg to meet Hitler.

A week later, on the night of 17 September, II./FJR 7 of 2. FJD dropped near Portoferraio on the island of Elba with the task of taking the city and the west side of the island. The next morning II./FJR 7 dropped on the southwest of the island, and Army troops landed by boat to secure the whole island and capture the Italian garrison. Allied troops recaptured most of the Aegean islands, but on 12 November, in a final fling, I./FJR 2, veterans of Crete and Corinth, dropped on Leros (in combination with a boat landing) and recaptured the island from the British.

The toughest battle in Italy was at Monte Cassino which was a major defence point on the Gustav Line blocking the way to Rome. The ad hoc Parachute Group *Schulz* (from FJR 1 and FJR 3) was among the original defenders from January 1944, but in March 1944 1. FJD took over the full defence responsibility, holding out in the rubble to which the monastery was largely reduced in the January–June 1944 period when it was under Allied attack. When Monte Cassino was first taken over, men of the *Hermann Göring* Division spent three weeks collecting up the archives and treasures from the monastery and moving them to safety at the Vatican and La Spoleta. Huge Allied efforts were needed to dislodge the defenders and outflank the position. Most of 1. FJD got away safely when the position was abandoned, and the depth of the walls and network of tunnels and dugouts in the ruins contributed to their survival from intense shelling and bombing.

The Anzio landing in January 1944 saw the first engagement of a new formation, 4. FJD which had been vested at Perugia in December from new regiments FJR 10, 11, and 12. This was made up of core personnel from 2. FJD, LLStR, and various Italian volunteers and men transferred from Luftwaffe field units. The commander was Oberst, later Generalmajor, Heinz Trettner. One battalion from each 4. FJD regiment joined with the *Hermann Göring* Panzer-Division and they held the beach head until Fourteenth Army arrived in strength. Fierce fighting ensued with 4. FJD in the thick of it until the Cassino battle flared up again in May.

THE FINAL YEARS

On paper the German airborne forces expanded considerably in the final 18 months of the war. Much of this was achieved by the decision to disband Luftwaffe field divisions and incorporate them into the airborne forces. In addition some other Luftwaffe personnel became available as the air element was reduced in size by attrition. Very little attempt was made at airborne training, for the new divisions were essentially ground fighting troops, but most of the new formations were leavened by veterans from the old days in core positions. They ensured that the airborne traditions were carried on by the new units. However, as the war came closer to its end some grandly named divisions were little more than scratch formations, often well under strength and sometimes reduced to a few battle groups.

In October 1943 3. Fallschirmjäger Division (3. FJD) was formed in France comprising FJR 5, 8, and 9. There were now four airborne divisions and in January 1944 they were organised into I. Fliegerkorps (1. and 4. FJD) based in Italy and II. Fliegerkorps (2. and 3. FJD) based in France. There was also the former Luftwaffe-manned *Hermann Göring* Panzer-Division which became in the new scheme of things the *Hermann Göring* Fallschirm Panzer-Division. Later a second Panzer division was formed and the two divisions formed the *Hermann Göring* Fallschirm Panzerkorps and were transferred to the Eastern Front in 1945.

Right: From a well-known sequence of photos, taken during a 1944 exercise in France; note the man on the left wears the standard ammunition bandolier.

Opposite, Above: Another scene from the same Normandy exercise.

Opposite, Below: Flak 88 next to a Marder II—a 7.5cm PaK on a Panzer II chassis.

Above: 9. FJD surrenders to the Russians in Berlin, May 1945. Note the Su-122 at left.

Left: Ramcke surrendering to the US Army at Brest on 20 September 1944.

Opposite, Above: The 'Hermann Göring' Fallschirm Panzerkorps attacking Soviet armour south of Bautzen on 22 April 1945—the last German victory on the Eastern Front.

Opposite, Below: Panthers of the Fallschirm Panzerkorps were attached to FJR 2 for a counter-attack near Kirovgrad in December 1943. Oberst Kroh, the regimental commander, is second from right.

In March 1944, Student, now a Generaloberst, was told to form all these elements into 1. Fallschirm-Armee, under control of C-in-C West. In September 1944 it came under control of Army Group B and was responsible for defence of the Low Countries. 5. FJD was formed at Rheims in March 1944, comprising FJR 13, 14 and 15 and fought in Normandy at St Lô and Caen but was largely wiped out in the Falaise Pocket. 6. FJD, comprising FJR 17 and 18, was a low strength division formed in Normandy in June 1944 and almost wiped out soon after. 7. FJD was a scratch formation got together hastily by Generalleutnant Erdmann, Student's chief of staff, largely to defend the line of the Albert Canal in September 1944, but some units were thrown into the Arnhem battle with some success. 8. FJD was another scratch division, much under strength, from assorted units which fought in defence of the homeland in the January–April 1945 period.

9. FJD was formed near Stettin in January 1945, with newly raised FJR 25, 26 and 27 and disparate units for service on the Eastern Front. It fought at Breslau and on the Oder and was involved in the defence of Berlin where it surrendered to the Russians in May 1945. 10. FJD was formed in February 1945 with some men pulled out of Italy before the surrender there. It was intended to go to the Dutch–German border with 1. Fallschirm-Armee, but then was switched to Austria instead, later moving into Moravia where it surrendered to the Russians. 11. FJD existed only on paper except for a few staff officers and its designated commander, Oberst Gericke. New regiments FJR 37, 38 and 39 were to be raised for service in Holland

Above and Right: Realistic training kept the Fallschirmjäger as a credible fighting force until well into 1945. These photos show various equipment and locations, including: Normandy 1944 (Above), MG34 in the LMG (bipod) role (right); manning a roadblock (centre right), and with an MP40 SMG (Bottom right).

Top right: Early war (note white canopies) training exercise.

in March 1945 but in the chaotic last few weeks of the war this never happened.

In the spring of 1944 two independent assault gun brigades, equipped with the Sturmgeschütz (StuG) III, were formed at Melun in France from airborne personnel, StuG-Brigade XI and StuG-Brigade XII. The former was transferred to the Eastern Front in the closing weeks of the war, but in 1944 they both acted in support of various airborne divisions fighting in the west including 5. FJD in the Ardennes and 7. FJD in defence of the Reich.

1. FJD and 4. FJD fought on in Italy until the final surrender of the forces there in April 1945. 2. FJD, under Ramcke, fought with distinction in Normandy, countering the US airborne divisions around Carentan, then in Brittany, and finally holding out at 'Fortress Brest' until September 1944. FJR 6 survived the surrender of 2. FJD, fought at Arnhem, and made the last German airborne drop of the war as part of the Ardennes Offensive in December 1944, though this was not a success and missed its objectives. The various 1. Fallschirm-Armee divisions fought at Arnhem and Nijmegen, took part in the defence of the Maas and the Waal, the Reichswald battle, the withdrawal to the Rhine, defence of the Rhinelands and the Ems and Weser withdrawal. The *Hermann Göring* Fallschirm Panzerkorps ended the war on the Eastern Front, mainly in East Saxony and lower Silesia. They were among the forces achieving the last German victory of the war, the recapture of Bautzen, and finally surrendering to the Russians near Dresden.

Above: MG.34 used in the heavy machine-gun role on a tripod, the carrying straps are clearly visible. The gun commander on the left carries the map case of an officer.

Left: A weapons container being carried out to a waiting aircraft. The concertina-like cylinder on the end is designed to take the impact on landing.

Right: The 27mm *Leuchtpistole* manufactured by Walther was used for signalling purposes. The four types of ammunition available were high explosive, smoke, indicator (ie signal flare) and single illuminating parachute flare. The man is wearing a flare cartridge bandolier. Note rank badge on right arm of camouflage smock.

CONSTITUENT UNITS OF THE FALLSCHIRMJÄGER DIVISIONS, APRIL 1943–APRIL 1945

1st Fallschirmjäger Division
Created out of 7. Flieger-Division April
1943 (CO Generalmajor Heidrich
promoted Generalleutnant during
1944)
FJR 1 (CO Oberst Schulz)
FJR 3 (CO Oberst Heilmann)
FJR 4 (CO Oberst Walther)
Fallschirm Artillery Regiment 1 (CO Major
Schram)
Fallschirm PzJg Battalion I
Fallschirm Pioneer Battalion I
Fallschirm Signals Battalion I
Fallschirm MG Battalion I
Fallschirm Medical Battalion I

2nd Fallschirmjäger Division
Raised Brittany 1943
(CO Generalleutnant Ramcke)
FJR 2 (CO Oberst Kroh)
FJR 6 (CO Major Liebach)
FJR 7 (CO Oberst Straub)
Fallschirm Artillery Regiment 2
Fallschirm PzJg Battalion II
Fallschirm Engineer Battalion II
Fallschirm Signals Battalion II
Fallschirm Medical Battalion II
Fallschirm Services Units
Fallschirm AA Bn II, Fallschirm Mortar Bn
II and Replacement Bn II raised Jan
1944

3nd Fallschirmjäger Division
Raised France 1943
(CO Generalmajor Schimpf)
FJR 5* (CO Major Becker)
FJR 8 (CO Major Liebach)
FJR 9 (CO Major Stephani)
Fallschirm Artillery Regiment 3
Fallschirm PzJg Battalion III
Fallschirm Pioneer Battalion III
Fallschirm AA Battalion III
Fallschirm Mortar Battalion III
Fallschirm Signals Battalion III

* FJR 5 lost in Africa (reconstituted it
became part of 3. FJD in March 1944

4th Fallschirmjäger Division
Raised Italy during Nov/Dec 1943
(CO Generalmajor Trettner)
FJR 10 (CO Oberst Fuchs)
FJR 11 (CO Major Gericke)

FJR 12 (CO Major Timm)
Fallschirm Artillery Regiment 4
Fallschirm PzJg Battalion IV
Fallschirm Pioneer Battalion IV
Fallschirm Signals Battalion IV
Also units from the Italian Divisions
'Folgore' and 'Demgo'

5th Fallschirmjäger Division
Rraised France April 1944
(CO Generalleutnant Wilke)
FJR 13 (CO Major von der Schulenburg)
FJR 14 (CO Major Noster)
FJR 15 (CO Major Groschke)
Fallschirm Artillery Regiment 5
Fallschirm PzJg Battalion V
Fallschirm Pioneer Battalion V
Fallschirm Mortar Battalion V
Fallschirm AA Battalion V
Fallschirm Signals Battalion V

6th Fallschirmjäger Division*
Raised Metz and Nancy April 1944
(CO Generalmajor von Heyking)
FJR 16 (CO Oberstleutnant Schirmer)
FJR 17
FJR 18
Fallschirm Artillery Regiment 6
Fallschirm PzJg Battalion VI
Fallschirm Mortar Battalion VI
Fallschirm AA Battalion VI
Fallschirm Pioneer Battalion VI
Fallschirm Signals Battalion No VI
Replacement Battalion
Reconnaissance Company

* Division re-raised around Kleve in the
Rhineland, end 1944, following
decimation in France and Belgium

(CO Generalmajor Plocher)
FJR 16 (CO Oberst Dorn (2 x battalions)
FJR 17 (CO Oberst Vetter)
FJR 18 (CO Major Witzig)
Fallschirm Artillery Regiment 6
Fallschirm PzJg Battalion VI
Fallschirm Mortar Battalion VI
Fallschirm AA Battalion VI
Fallschirm Pioneer Battalion VI
Fallschirm Signals Battalion No VI
Replacement Battalion
Reconnaissance Company

7th Fallschirmjäger Division
Raised Belgium September 1944
(CO Generalleutnant Erdmann)
FJR 19 (CO Oberst Menzel)
FJR 20 (CO Oberstleutnant Grassmel)
FJR 21 (CO Oberst Loytweg-Hardegg)
Fallschirm Artillery Regiment 7
Fallschirm PzJg Battalion VII
Fallschirm Pioneer Battalion VII
Fallschirm Mortar Battalion VII
Fallschirm Signals Battalion VII
Divisional Units

8th Fallschirmjäger Division
Raised January 1945
(CO Generalmajor Wadehan)
FJR 22 (CO Oberstleutnant von der
Tanne)
FJR 23 (served with 2nd Division from
November 1944)
FJR 24 (CO Oberstleutnant Hübner)
Pioneer Battalion VIII
Replacement Battalion
Divisional supply units

9th Fallschirmjäger Division
Raised south of Stettin
(CO Generalleutnant Wilke)
FJR 25 (CO Major Schact)
FJR 26 (CO Major Brede)
FJR 27 (CO Major Abratis)
Fallschirm Artillery Regiment 9
Fallschirm PzJg Battalion IX
Fallschirm Pioneer Battalion IX
Fallschirm AA Battalion IX
Fallschirm Signals Battalion No 9

10th Fallschirmjaeger Division
Raised February 1945 in eastern Austria
(CO Oberst von Hoffmann)
FJR 28 (CO Major Schmucker)
FJR 29 (CO Major Genz)
FJR 30 (CO Oberstleutnant Wolff)
Fallschirm Artillery Regiment 10
Fallschirm Pioneer Battalion X
Fallschirm PzJg Battalion X

11th Fallschirmjäger Division
This division was set up and used
piecemeal in March 1945
(CO Oberst Gericke). Intended
regiments—FJR 37, 38 and 39

EQUIPMENT & MARKINGS

Above: Paras inside a Ju 52.

Opposite: After landing a fully-equipped Fallschirmjager disengages his harness. Although this man is wearing a Luftwaffe jump suit he is also wearing an Army eagle on his right breast.

Previous page: Paratrooper in second model smock with FG42 assault rifle. The re-enactment colour photographs in this chapter are by Daniel Peterson and reproduced by kind permission of the photographer.

The specialised fighting function of the airborne troops required combat clothing and equipment – and in some cases weapons – adapted to the role, and there were modes of use, also, not previously encountered in conventional ground fighting.

UNIFORMS

Temperate Areas

In Europe standard Luftwaffe service dress and head-dress was worn for parades, walking out, leave and general duties, with the usual Luftwaffe practice of substituting the simplified *Fliegerbluse* in place of the tunic for work wear, combat, or even walking out, at regimental discretion. The appropriate arm-of-service colour (*Waffenfarbe*) was incorporated in head-dress piping, rank badges, and shoulder straps and for paratroops this was golden yellow except for specialist troops such as signallers, engineers, medical attendants, etc., who wore the colour of their branch.

For combat, however, paratroops wore very distinctive specialised clothing, the most revolutionary item, for the time, being the jump smock. The original pattern was of the step-in type. This smock was made in a field-grey (green-grey) drill material and was the pattern originally developed for the Army parachute battalion. It continued in wear after the battalion was transferred to the Luftwaffe. The Army pattern national eagle badge was worn on the right breast and veterans of the Army parachute battalion proudly wore this well into their time of service as Luftwaffe personnel. Despite the original intention that the smock would be discarded for ground combat, it was found to be a good utilitarian garment in its own right and those issued with it mostly retained it in combat. It was secured by two vertical full-length exposed zips arranged so that the front panel came out completely, allowing quick removal on landing, for the original thinking was that this smock would be worn for jumping only, covering personal equipment, and would be discarded once on the ground. The smock had a band that fastened at the neck and tight press-studded cuffs. Zips in the side of the smock gave access through to the trouser pockets.

The Luftwaffe's original smock design was also in grey-green drill, though some were also made in blue-grey, particularly in the early years. This smock also had 'step in' legs at thigh height, but it had a conventional buttoned fly front (soon

replaced by a zip) and a conventional fall collar. It also had side slits to give access to trouser pockets, and the Luftwaffe version of the national eagle emblem was worn on the right breast. To make it more suited to combat wear it was soon modified to give two diagonally-zipped breast pockets and two at thigh level, though there were a number of variations in pocket size and positioning in the 1940 period while the optimum arrangement was developed. Some smocks at this time had only two pockets.

As with the Army pattern smock, the Luftwaffe smock was worn over personal equipment when jumping, and then had to be removed or the personal equipment transferred to the outside once the man was on the ground.

The parachute combat trousers were gathered in at the ankles and had conventional side and (two) hip pockets, plus a fob pocket at the front. However, they also had long slits on each outer seam at knee height, secured by press studs. These gave access to allow removal of the knee pads, worn under the trousers when jumping. Knee pads worn outside the trousers were additional to these. An interior pocket inside the right hand slit held the special paratrooper's knife (primarily designed for emergency release of the parachute lines on the ground), and this had a blade which slid in and out of the handle.

Jump boots were of black leather, heavily reinforced and rubber-soled. The tops came well above the ankle and covered the gathered-in trouser bottoms. Early boots had side lacing, but later the pattern was changed to conventional front lacing. When emphasis changed to ground fighting after 1941, many men wore conventional service leather ankle boots, in black or brown depending on source, sometimes with canvas or cloth anklets. When jumping the paratroops wore long black leather gauntlets with elasticated tops.

By early 1941 (and first worn in action in Crete), a new 'second pattern' jump smock was being issued. It differed from the earlier pattern in eliminating the 'step in' legs. Instead the skirt was fitted with press studs so that it could be secured tightly round the thighs when jumping, then loosened to form a conventional jacket shape in action. Some of these new smocks were produced in plain olive green, but most were in 'splinter' camouflage pattern. A cloth helmet cover in the same camouflage pattern was also issued, as were some in plain olive green. This 'second pattern' smock was broadly copied in style for British paratroops.

The abbreviated helmet was unique to parachute units, and distinctive as a recognition feature for troops on the ground. The design was intended to eliminate the chances of catching on aircraft fittings and doorways, etc., or on branches or ground objects as the paratrooper landed. The original version developed for the first Army paratroopers was based on the standard Model 1935 German military helmet, reduced in depth all round by taking about 2cm off the rim. The liner was beefed up and the single chin strap was replaced by strong Y-straps. Distinctive was a small horizontal slot on each side just above the rim. The Luftwaffe pattern helmet, which became universal, was similar to the Army design, but without the small side slots and with a slightly more prominent rim. When new, helmets carried a shield decal in national colours (black/white/red) on the right side and

Below: Parachute sergeant with full equipment—MP38 machine-pistol, six magazines pouches, binoculars, water bottle with cup. His rank badge is on his left arm (see page 80).

Left: Early Fallschirmjäger attire. TRH Pictures

Below left and right: The second model parachutist's jump smock in Luftwaffe *Splittermuster*. It is seen here with matching helmet cover and bandolier for the K98 Mauser rifle. The bandolier holds 20 five-round clips of ammunition.

the Army pattern eagle decal (original Army parachute units only) or a Luftwaffe pattern national eagle on the left side. Later in the war these decals were commonly omitted, or painted over, or smeared over with mud to reduce their prominence. From 1941 cloth helmet covers were issued, as previously noted, but also used on helmets were elasticated bands, string netting, or even wire netting, to hold foliage as camouflage.

Many items of Army issue, such as smocks, boots, or even helmets of ordinary service pattern could be seen in wear later in the war, and pictorial evidence suggests that even in the early months of the war some men were issued with conventional service helmets while paratroop helmets were in short supply. On the Eastern Front in cold weather, parachute units wore conventional Army style winter combat clothing, notably the reversible (white/olive green) padded smock and trousers.

Tropical Clothing

When the war started the Luftwaffe had no specific tropical clothing, and the first Luftwaffe air squadron personnel who went to North Africa in early 1941 wore Army issue tropical uniforms with Luftwaffe badges and insignia. Specific Luftwaffe items were soon developed, however, notably a tropical tunic which was similar in pattern and style to the ordinary service tunic except that it was slightly looser in cut and was made of biscuit colour cotton drill with brown metal buttons. A specific tropical issue tunic, even fuller in cut, was designed for paratroops, obviously intended to replace the smock. It had the breast pockets replaced by bandolier holders kept in place by brown metal press studs. These were to be troop-tested by the *Ramcke* Brigade in 1942, prior to general issue, but when parachute landings were discontinued there was no further production, though the test tunics remained in use by some *Ramcke* Brigade members. In practice paratroops in tropical dress kept their standard smocks for wear as required.

Below: Paras on Crete. Note camouflage smocks and pistols.

Matching tropical trousers had a built-in belt, with straps to gather in the bottoms of the legs, tight to the ankles or boots, giving a full cut baggy effect. A deep patch pocket with flap was on the left thigh front, plus the usual trouser side pockets. The matching shorts were in similar style but without the patch pocket. All these garments were made in beige or biscuit colour cotton drill which soon faded or washed out to a light stone shade. While canvas/leather high boots and short brown leather boots were issued for tropical wear, most paratroops preferred to wear their issue jump boots.

The tropical shirt had two pleated breast pockets and a cloth Luftwaffe eagle breast badge. Brown metal buttons were fitted. It came in long or short sleeve versions, was quite loosely cut, and was made of tan cotton drill which, like the other garments, usually faded to a lighter shade. This variation in fading between different items of clothing often gave a 'patchy' appearance to groups of men in tropical clothing.

Issued to paratroops sent to North Africa was the Luftwaffe tropical helmet, made in pith with a tan/beige cloth covering and red inside lining in the crown and green lining under the rim. It had a brown leather chin strap and was similar to the Army pattern except for a narrower more angled brim and a Luftwaffe metal eagle badge on the left side. A shield in the national colours was carried on the right side. Most distinctive of all was the Luftwaffe tropical cap, a soft full crowned, wide peaked cap in beige drill with a button-on cloth neck cover which could be added as required. It also had a chin strap that could be worn down or up. It was issued from May 1942. Also worn was the tropical version of the Army pattern soft peaked *Feldmütze* forage cap with the Luftwaffe eagle emblem, either in cloth or metal, added, and this was mainly taken up before the Luftwaffe tropical cap was on issue. Finally, in 1941, was issued a tropical version of the fore-and-aft *Fliegermütze* forage cap, again in beige drill.

It should be noted that in cold weather in areas where tropical dress was ordered, the standard European issue Luftwaffe blue overcoat was worn, as were other items of European issue clothing, such as head wear and the smock, when the situation justified it.

Above: The workhorse of the Luftwaffe was the Junkers Ju 52, from whose familiar corrugated shell the Fallschirmjäger exited in diving position.

BADGES AND INSIGNIA

Aside from the standard badges and distinctions of rank worn with Luftwaffe service dress, there were special rank badges for camouflage clothing, introduced for wear on the smock in 1940, though initially only slowly issued. The rank badges duplicated the pattern of stylised wings and bars already in use on Luftwaffe flying suits. The symbols were in white on a grey-green patch worn on each upper arm of the smock. Generals had the symbols in gold instead of white. These badges gave a very logical and distinctive method or recognising rank and command in combat without being too prominent to enemy eyes. Prior to full issue of these special cloth rank badges, officers and men either carried no visible rank badges on their smocks, or transferred the standard rank badges from their service dress.

Also worn, and intended for service dress, were commemorative cuff titles, worn on the left cuff. Sometimes they were seen on smock cuffs also, though this appears to have been an unofficial application. Most famous was the *Kreta* title in yellow and white which was issued to all who took part in the invasion of Crete. Less common was *Afrika* for men, such as those of *Ramcke* Brigade, who served in Cyrenaica, Libya, or Tunis. Some regiments or divisions also had cuff titles, notably *Fallschirm-Jäger 1* issued in 1939, and some subsequent variations and manifestations of the regiments and divisions named for Reichsmarschall Göring.

To qualify as a parachutist a trainee had to complete six jumps successfully. He was then awarded the parachutist badge which was worn on the left breast. The Army badge featured a diving eagle on a laurel wreath with a Nazi eagle and swastika let into the top. The Luftwaffe badge had the diving eagle clasping a swastika in its talons superimposed over a simpler laurel wreath. Former Army parachutists proudly wore the Army badge instead of the Luftwaffe version for years after their transfer to the Luftwaffe.

As the parachute force expanded in the war years, several of the divisions adopted formation signs similar to the Army type. These were as follows:

1. Fallschirmjäger-Division   A green devil astride a red trident, superimposed on a white square. The post-war (1956 onwards) 1st Parachute Division had a white parachute symbol, superimposed on a blue square, and this was also worn as a badge on the upper left sleeve of the uniform.

2. Fallschirmjäger-Division   This was formed in 1942, initially as a brigade known as *Ramcke* Brigade after its commander, and in this form it saw service in North Africa in 1942, before moving to Italy and being reorganised as a division. In both manifestations the formation sign was a kite outline with a large R inside

Below: Unlike Allied forces, German paras dropped without equipment. Here is a early war view of a para ready to drop as exemplified by German boxing champion Max Schmeling.

Above left and right: Grenade bags for the Steilhandgranate Models 1939 and 1943. As these are manufactured in the Luftwaffe *Splittermuster* it is highly likely that they were a specialised equipment item for paratroopers, and possibly for Luftwaffe Field Division troops. Barely discernible is the black webbing strap connecting the top inner corners of the bags behind the neck; a second strap across the small of the back connects the bottom corners. The distinctive Luftwaffe splinter camouflage pattern is printed on one side of the cloth only.

Left: Further view of the second model 'bone sack', this time with the bandolier for the paratroopers' FG42 assault rifle. Each pocket carries one 20-round box magazine, totalling 160 rounds.

Opposite, from top to bottom: Emblems were introduced later in the war for some para units. These are:

1	1. FJD
2	2. FJD (or Brigade Ramcke)
3	4. FJD
4	22nd Luftlande Division
5	Postwar 1. FJD para badge (from 1956)

it signifying its commander, General Ramcke. A subsidiary initial (K, vH, H, B) indicated the different regimental commanders according to sub-unit. The sign was usually in black on a white rectangle. The initials indicated the following battalion commanders: K – Kroh or Kargerer, vH – von der Heydte, H – Hübner, B – Burckhardt. The subsidiary initial was not always carried.

4. Fallschirmjäger-Division   This formation had a stylised 'comet' of a white outline star with a blue/red/blue 'flaring' tail, on a white square. Sometimes the star/tail symbol was used in a simplified solid colour (white, red, blue, etc.) without the background.

22. (Luftlande) Panzergrenadier-Division   In the early part of the war up to the Crete operation this was the designated Army air-landing division which worked with 7. Flieger-Division. Its sign was a shield with red/white vertical stripes and a horizontal bar in red/white checks, derived from the state flag of Bremen.

These formation signs could be seen placed variously on front, back, or sides of divisional vehicles though pictorial evidence suggests they were not nearly so frequently applied as formation signs on Army or Waffen-SS vehicles. Where appropriate, Army style tac signs to indicate type of unit could also be seen displayed when divisions fought as ground troops, but again they do not seem to have been so often applied as on Army vehicles. Vehicles also carried a military number plate either painted directly or affixed on front and rear with the index letters WL – Wehrmacht Luftwaffe – prefixing the number. Lettering was black on white.

WEAPONS AND TRANSPORT

While parachute troops were equipped with the standard range of small arms and support weapons used by ground troops, when used in airborne operations there were limitations in artillery and anti-tank weapons they could use since all equipment had to be light enough to be transported by air, and preferably capable of being dropped by parachute as well. The principal equipments used were as follows:

Anti-tank Weapons
Panzerbüsche 39   This was the most recent version of the rifle calibre (7.92mm) anti-tank rifle which had long been used by the Army but was obsolescent when the war started. Its best performance was penetrating 30mm of armour at 100 metre range (1.2in/110yd), so it was inadequate except against light armoured vehicles at close range. Nonetheless it was used in action in the 1940–41 period. It had the advantage of being man-portable.
Panzerbüsche 42   This replaced the Panzerbüsche 39 in 1942 and was a lightened version of the similar 2.8cm taper-bore weapon produced for the Army. It had a tubular steel carriage with small tyred wheels. While the calibre was the same as the Army equivalent the barrel and muzzle velocity were much improved to give a 400 metre range and best penetration of 55mm of armour (2.2in/440yd). This was at the expense of barrel wear, with a barrel life of only 500 rounds. The gun could traverse 25 degrees either side on the carriage, and the weapon could be broken into five parts for parachuting.
PaK 36   This was the standard 3.7cm light anti-tank gun widely used by ground troops, but the largest gun that could be carried inside a Ju 52, weighing in at 450kg (990lb). It could not be broken down and initially could only be delivered

Above: Cuff title and Fallschirmjäger breast badge.

as part of an air-landing operation. However, experiments showed that it could be carried between the undercarriage legs of a Ju 52 and delivered below five parachutes. In this form it was used in later operations. On the ground it could only be hauled by hand, but it was then discovered that it could be pulled by the BMW or Zündapp 750cc motor-cycle combinations also used by the parachute troops, and this became the mode of transport, but the gun team had to be restricted to four men to allow this.

Support Artillery

Gebirgskanone 15   Initially the lightest artillery piece available for the support role was the obsolescent Czech Skoda-built 7.5cm Gebirgskanone 15 which had been designed for mountain troop use. It weighed 630kg (1,390lb) and broke down into seven parts and could be carried and air-landed inside a Ju 52. It still had to be hauled on the ground and it was decided to use small Haflinger horses for this which could also be carried inside the Ju 52. The guns and horse teams were deployed in the air landing in Holland on 10 May 1940, but this proved to be a fiasco as the horses stampeded under fire as they landed. The scheme was abandoned and not used again. Subsequently a few of the later 7.5cm **Gebirgsgeschütze 36** were used, but they were heavier at 750kg (1,650lb) and broke into eight components that had to be carried.

kurzer Granatwerfer 42   Initially the paratroops used the standard 8.1cm German infantry mortars, but in 1940 a special short mortar (the 'Stummelwerfer') was developed specially for airborne use. With a barrel length of 747mm (29.5in), and breaking into three loads each around 18kg (40lb) in weight, it was compact and very portable. It could also be fired at a distance using a lanyard attached to the firing bolt. In service in 1941 it was popular and effective and was also later taken up by the Army and Waffen-SS.

Recoilless Weapons

The air-portable artillery problem was to some extent ameliorated by the production of recoilless guns, which the firms of Krupp and Rheinmetall had both been developing in the late 1930s. Even before the war started they had been asked for lightweight designs for airborne use. By 1940 the first of these, the Krupp 7.5cm LG 1, was in limited service and was first used in action during the invasion of Crete. (LG = leichte Geschütze = light gun). To keep the weight down it had a simple tubular carriage and spoked bicycle-type wheels. This proved a weak point, with some carriages literally collapsing in action. Rheinmetall took over the design and produced a beefed up version, the 7.5cm LG 40 with a much stronger carriage and smaller metal disc tyred wheels. These could be removed and the carriage could then be emplaced in tripod form. Some 450 were produced and the LG 40 was used in Crete. The LG 40 could be dropped by parachute in four component parts, but containers were preferred in order to ensure all the parts arrived together. An experienced crew could assemble the gun in about two minutes. Some LG 1s were dropped in component parts in wicker baskets. LG 40 range was 6,500 metres (7,100yd), rate of fire 6 rounds per minute.

To give even more punch both Krupp and Rheinmetall produced 10.5cm weapons in 1941–42, the 10.5cm LG 40

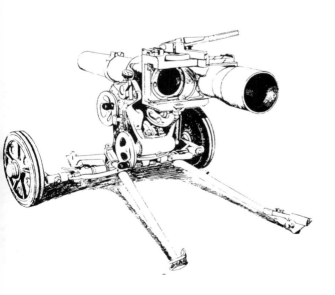

(confusingly with the same designation as Krupp's 7.5cm) and the 10.5cm LG 42 (Rheinmetall). Both could be towed by the muzzle, had blast shields, and larger metal tyred wheels, and could be emplaced by removing the wheels. Range was 8,000 metres (8,750yd). These weapons saw relatively limited service, however, because parachute operations were abandoned after Crete. The same fate was suffered by a later development, the 10.5cm LG 43 of 1943, an improved design that was made lighter and more portable for airborne use. When paratroop formations were used in the ground fighting role in the later part of the war they used the same artillery equipment as the Army, such as the PaK 40, PaK 75, etc.

Anti-aircraft Weapons

Initially the parachute flak battalions had the Fla-MG 15 which could be mounted on the motor-cycle combinations, and the widely used 2cm Flak 30 which in its airborne form had the shield removed. This could be towed on its two-wheel carriage by the motor-cycle combination, and could also be broken into six components for manhandling. This weapon had to be carried into an air-landing inside a Ju 52 but some are said to have be dropped by parachute cluster from under a Ju 52. To overcome this problem the 2cm Gebirgsflak 38 was designed with weight in action reduced from the Flak 30's 463kg (1,020lb) to 276kg (608lb) and overall weight only 315kg (694lb). This was an excellent compact design for use both by mountain and airborne troops and it could be para-dropped with its two-wheel carriage from beneath a Ju 52. However, it only saw limited service with the airborne forces since the need for it was gone by the time it was ready.

Above: The standard airborne light mortar (8cm kurzer Granatenwerfer 42)—specially developed for airborne forces.

Vehicles

Vehicles specifically used in airborne operations were the BMW R12 motorcycle, solo or with sidecars, the BMW R75, and the Zündapp KS750, both with sidecars with driven axles. These could tow the airborne artillery pieces as noted above and carry minimal gun crews. They also towed ammunition trailers. All could be carried inside a Ju 52 but early experiments established that they could also be dropped by parachute cluster. Unique was the NSU Kettenkrad half-track motor-cycle which was designed for airborne use and first employed on Crete. This was an extremely useful towing and load-carrying vehicle which could be carried under a Ju 52 or inside the larger gliders.

Containers

Small arms and ammunition in airborne operations were dropped separately in the containers previously mentioned. This was unsatisfactory because parachutists could be engaged by waiting defenders (as in Crete) before they could recover their personal arms from the container. Because of this limitation there were several recorded cases where men ignored the official procedure and carried their small arms with them when they dropped, usually an MP38 or MP40 sub-machine gun, or a rifle, sometimes padded or wrapped in canvas attached to the parachute harness, so that they could go into action immediately on landing. A special item developed was the canvas bandolier carrying up to 200 rounds that could be slung round the neck beneath the smock when jumping. Containers also carried food, medical stores, and radio or pioneer equipment, etc. The later versions had small wheels and a tow handle fitted, these being put in place after the containers were

Below: Parachute riflemen taking arms including MG34 LMG and MP38 machine pistols from an arms container. The metal end of the container has been crumpled on the impact of landing. Note colour-coded container markings.

Left: Detail of right rear panel of a midwar jump smock in *Sumpfmuster*, showing the buttoned fastening of the flare pistol holster, tightening snap, and holes for the metal belt support hooks. The well-used snap has lost its green-grey baked enamel finish, leaving the brass exposed.

Below left and right: The parachutist's jump smock in Luftwaffe *Sumpfmuster*, a special pattern which seems to have been created by modifying the printing rollers originally used to print the air force splinter pattern. It is manufactured from a double-faced twill cotton/rayon blend offering excellent wind resistance. Note the charcteristic jump smock pocket details; and the skirt fastened into separate 'legs' by press studs.

Above right: Tunisia, 1943, with sand-coloured helmet and Luftwaffe tropical trousers. This midwar production jump smock is still made of predominantly cotton blend with rayon and weave identical to that employed in the *Zeltbahn*.

Below right: DFS 230 gliders.

recovered so that they could be used as battlefield barrows. Colour coding and smoke markers were used to help the troops locate their particular containers once on the ground, but the system was wasteful and vulnerable, for it needed four containers for every 12 men as a rule of thumb which took up a lot of payload space. And to compensate for containers going astray it was necessary to drop up to twice the quantity of small arms and ammunition than would be needed by an equivalent ground force.

Gliders

As already noted the DFS 230 was the standard assault glider. This was towed by the Ju 52. A Ju 52 could tow up to three gliders of this type at a time, but in actual airborne assaults only one was towed. The special unit formed to tow the glider assault regiment was known as the Luftlandegeschwader. At the time of the Crete invasion this required 192 Ju 52s to take the entire assault regiment into action. Ten men were carried in one glider, and one platoon needed three gliders. A battalion of 480 men therefore required 48 gliders and 48 tugs and a Luftlandesgruppe of 48 aircraft was allocated to each battalion. Subsequent to the Crete campaign there were no more actual airborne assaults, but the DFS 230 glider and the larger Gotha 242 were used by the airborne forces to transport their men and equipment between various operational fronts such as Tunis and Sicily or Italy and France. However, these were not specifically allocated to airborne forces, and the gliders were also used for general supply and personnel carrier work. Later the giant Messerschmitt 323 was used in the same role.

Above: Paras after the fall of Eben Emael.

Below: Badges worn on Fliegerbluse or camouflage smocks—blue-grey background, generals with gold insignia, otherwise white.

Right: Army or Luftwaffe para in fighting order. Drawings from US official recognition charts.

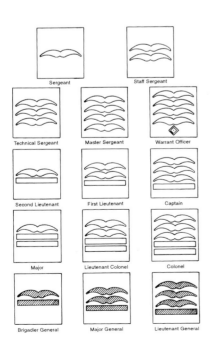

Sergeant

Staff Sergeant

Technical Sergeant

Master Sergeant

Warrant Officer

Second Lieutenant

First Lieutenant

Captain

Major

Lieutenant Colonel

Colonel

Brigadier General

Major General

Lieutenant General

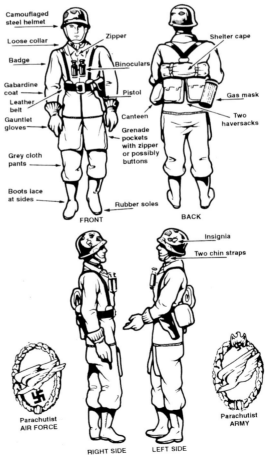

Camouflaged steel helmet

Loose collar

Badge

Gabardine coat

Leather belt

Gauntlet gloves

Grey cloth pants

Boots lace at sides

Zipper

Binoculars

Pistol

Canteen

Grenade pockets with zipper or possibly buttons

Rubber soles

FRONT

Shelter cape

Gas mask

Two haversacks

BACK

Insignia

Two chin straps

RIGHT SIDE

LEFT SIDE

Parachutist AIR FORCE

Parachutist ARMY

Left: Officers attending an anti-tank course. The 3.7cm PaK36 was the largest anti-tank gun to be air-dropped by the Germans.

Below left: Early war view of para ready to jump, with static line over his shoulder.

Below: The Gigant glider was adapted later in the war to become a heavy transport.

PEOPLE

Above: General Student, the Luftwaffe commander for the invasion of Crete.

GENERALFELDMARSCHAL ALBERT KESSELRING

Born 20 November 1885, Kesselring joined the German Army in 1904. By the end of World War I he was an experienced staff officer. When the Luftwaffe was formed in 1935 he transferred from the Army and was made Chief of Staff of the Luftwaffe after the death of the original post holder. While he was never directly involved at divisional or corps level with 7. Flieger or the airborne forces generally, he did exercise overall control in his various senior command posts. As Chief of Staff he sanctioned the original expansion of the airborne force and the development of its equipment in the late 1930s. As commander of Luftflotte II in 1940, 7. Flieger came under his overall control, just as it (and its expanded successors) did in 1941–45 when he was C-in-C South covering the whole Mediterranean area including North Africa, Italy and the Aegean. He was imprisoned for war crimes (a reprisal killing of Italian civilians) 1947–52, and died in July 1960.

GENERALOBERST DER FLIEGER KURT STUDENT

Born on 12 May 1890, Student finished cadre school training in 1910 and served in the infantry until 1914. He transferred to the fledgling air arm and by 1916 was a squadron commander, giving distinguished service until 1918. In the peacetime Reichswehr he served as Secretary for Technical Development in the Ministry for Aviation (1919–28) before returning to the infantry, first as company commander, then as a battalion commander. When the new Reichs Air Ministry was formed under the Nazi regime in 1933 he became commander of the new aviation test centres, then, as Generalmajor, Inspector General for Luftwaffe Training Schools, which included the parachute school at Stendal. When the airborne forces were expanded in 1938 he was appointed as first commander of 7. Flieger-Division. He retained command of all German airborne forces until 1945 as divisional, corps and army commander as they expanded throughout the war. He died in 1978.

GENERAL DER FALLSCHIRMTRUPPE BERNHARD RAMCKE

Ramcke was the most highly decorated German paratrooper of World War II, and was only the 20th Wehrmacht member to be awarded the Knights Cross with Oak Leaves, Swords, and Diamonds. This came in September 1944 after his doughty defence of 'Fortress Brest'. He had been awarded the DSC as a young NCO in World

War I. He first came to prominence with the airborne forces in 1941. He was by then a colonel on Student's staff, initially liaison officer with the air landing division, but he was called upon at Crete to jump in to replace the injured commander of the air landing assault regiment, After hard fighting in Crete he went to Italy to lead a training mission setting up Italian airborne forces. From there he was nominated to lead the German airborne forces in the projected invasion of Malta in 1942, but when this was cancelled he took his brigade to North Africa to reinforce Rommel's hard pressed *Afrika Korps*. After inspiring leadership there he left Tunis and returned to Europe where he led 2. FJD, most notably and finally as the defender of Brest in 1944.

GENERAL DER FALLSCHIRMTRUPPE EUGEN MEINDL

Meindl commanded the air landing assault regiment on Crete but was badly wounded soon after landing. When II. Fallschirmkorps was formed in 1944, Meindl became corps commander in the rank of General der Fallschirmtruppe.

GENERALLEUTNANT PETERSEN

Petersen was an Army officer who transferred to the Luftwaffe to command 7. Flieger-Division after the death of Walter Süssmann. In this position he led the division in operations on the Russian Front until October 1941 when succeeded by Generalmajor R. Heidrich.

GENERALMAJOR HEINZ TRETTNER

Trettner was Student's original chief of staff, a post he held for some years. He was one of Germany's most experienced airborne forces officers. When 4. FJD was formed he became its commander. Post-war he was the third Inspector General of the Bundeswehr.

GENERALLEUTNANT RICHARD HEIDRICH

Nicknamed 'Arno', Heidrich was older than most generals, tough but fatherly. He took over 7. Flieger from General Petersen and led it through the remaining Russian fighting, then on to Italy where he commanded the division (soon renamed 1.FJD) in their famous defence of Cassino. He died late in 1947.

Above: General Student making a point to a para in early 1941. Behind Student is von Roon (Staff of XI. Fliegerkorps). Note second mark of parachute RZ20.

Below: General der Fallschirmtruppe Ramcke as commander of Fortress Brest 19 September 1944 after his award of the Knight's Cross with Oakleaves, Swords and Diamonds.

FALLSCHIRMJÄGER RITTERKREUZTRÄGER

Eichenlaub mit Schwertern und Brillanten zum Ritterkreuz des Eisernen Kreuzes (in date order)

Ramcke, Bernhard-Hermann	19 Sept 44

Eichenlaub mit Schwertern zum Ritterrkeuz des Eisernen Kreuzes

Heidrich, Richard	25 Mar 44
Heilmann, Ludwig	15 May 44
Kroh, Johannes	12 Sept 44
Ramcke, Bernhard-Hermann	19 Sept 44
Schulz, Karl-Lothar	18 Nov 44
Walther, Erich	1 Feb 45
Meindl, Eugen	8 May 45

Eichenlaub zum Ritterkreuz des Eisernen Kreuzes

Ramcke, Bernhard-Hermann	13 Nov 42
Conrath, Paul	21 Aug 43
Student, Kurt	27 Sept 43
Schmalz, Wilhelm	23 Dec 43
Heidrich, Richard	5 Feb 44
Walther, Erich	2 Mar 44
Heilmann, Ludwig	2 Mar 44

Kroh, Johannes	6 Apr 44
Schulz, Karl-Lothar	20 Apr 44
Egger, Reinhard	24 June 44
Fitz, Josef	24 June 44
Meindl, Eugen	31 Aug 44
Pietzonka, Erich	16 Sept 44
Gericke, Walter	7 Sept 44
Trettner, Heinrich	17 Sept 44
Freiherr v d Heyde, Friedrich-August	30 Sept 44
Meyer, Heinz	18 Nov 44
Schirmer, Gerhard	18 Nov 44
Witzig, Rudolf	25 Nov 44
Rennecke, Rudolf	25 Nov 44
Gröschke, Kurt	9 Jan 45
Rossmann, Kari	1 Feb 45
von Baer, Bern	28 Feb 45
Becker, Kari-Heinz	12 Mar 45
Ostermeier, Hans	15 April 45
Veth, Kurt Major	30 April 45
Gortz, Helmut	30 April 45
Plocher, Hermann	8 May 45
Grassmel, Franz	8 May 45

Ritterkreuz des Eisernen Kreuzes (in alphabetic order)

24 Oct 44	Abratis, Herbert	1. FJD	12 May 40	Altmann, Gustav	1. FJD
20 July 43	Adolff, Paul	1. FJD	4 Dec 42	Arent, Peter	1. FJD
			13 May 40	Arpke, Helmut	1. FJD

9 July 41	Barmetler, Josef	7. Flieger-Div	30 Nov 44	Grunhold, Werner	FPzD 'HG'
21 Mar 45	Bausch, Friedrich	5. FJD	9 July 41	Hagl, Andreas	1. FJD
9 July 41	Becker, Karl-Heinz	1. FJD	9 June 44	Hahn, Constantin	FPzD 'HG'
5 Sept 44	Beine, Erich	4. FJD	5 Sept 44	Hamer, Heino	2. FJD
30 Sept 44	Bellinger, Hans-Joachim	FPzD 'HG'	11 Feb 45	Hansen, Hans-Christian	FPzGD 2 'HG'
27 Nov 44	Berg, Hartmut von	3. FJD	23 Feb 45	Hartelt, Wolfgang -	FPzD 'HG'
7 Feb 45	Berger, Karl	5. FJD	5 Sept 44	Hauber, Friedrich	4. FJD
15 Mar 45	Berneike, Rudolf	5. FJD	14 June 41	Heidrich, Richard	1. FJD
9 May 45	Behre, Friedrich	FPzD 'HG'	14 June 41	Heilmann, Ludwig	1. FJD
28 Mar 45	Bertram, ?	FPzD 'HG'	6 Oct 44	Hellmann, Erich	1. FJD
9 June 44	Beyer, Herbert	1. FJD	28 Apr 45	Hengstler, Richard	FstGBrig 12
18 Oct 44	Birnbaum, Fritz	FPzD 'HG'	9 July 41	Herrmann, Harry	1. FJD
29 Oct 44	Blauensteiner, Ernst	II. FsKorps	24 June 44	Heydenbreck, Georg-Henning von	FPzD 'HG'
24 May 40	Blücher, Wolfgang, Graf von	1. FJD	9 July 41	Freiherr v d Heyde, Friedrich-August	1. FJD
30 Nov 44	Boehlein, Rudolf	1. FJD	13 Sept 44	Herzbach, Max	2. FJD
26 Mar 44	Böhmler, Rudolf	1. FJD	18 May 43	Hoefeld, Robert	4./FJR 5
24 May 40	Bräuer, Bruno	1. FJD	1 Mar 45	Hönscheid, Hans	Kriegsberichter
14 Jan 45	Briegel, Hans	FPzD 'HG'	9 May 45	Hübner, Eduard	1. Fs-Armee
27 April 45	Büttner, Manfred	9. FJD	23 Nov 41	Itzen, Dirk	FlaRegt 'HG'
4 Sept 41	Conrath, Paul	FlaRegt 'HG'	13 Sept 44	Jacob, Rupert	2. FJD
7 Feb 45	Le Courte, Georg,	2. FJD	15 May 40	Jäger, Rolf	1. FJD
12 May 40	Delica, Egon	1. FJD	9 June 44	Jamrowski, Siegfried	1. FJD
28 Apr 45	Deutsch, Heinz	FstGBrig 12	9 May 45	Jungwirth, Hans	1. Fs-Armee
14 Jan 45	Donth, Rudolf	1. FJD	29 Oct 44	Kalow, Siegfried	FPzD 'HG'
9 July 41	Egger, Remhard	1. FJD	7 Feb45	Kampmann, ?	FPzGD 2 'HG'
29 Feb 44	Engelhardt, Johann	2. FJD	21 Aug 41	Kempke, Wilhelm	7. FJD
8 Feb 45	Erdmann, Wolfgang	7. FJD	24 May 40	Kerfin, Horst	1. FJD
17 Sept 44	Ewald, Werner	2. FJD	2 Feb 45	Kerutt, Hellmut	7. FJD
9 June 44	Foltin, Ferdinand	1. FJD	18 May 43	Kiefer Eduard	FPzD 'HG'
20 Oct 44	Francois, Edmund	FPzD 'HG'	12 May 40	Kiess, Walter	1. FJD
5 Sept 44	Fries, Herbert	1. FJD	2 Aug 43	Kluge, Walter	FPzD 'HG'
18 Nov 44	Frömming, Ernst	1 FJD	5 Apr 44	Knaf, Walter	FPzD 'HG'
14 June 41	Fulda, Wilhelm	1. FJD	24 Oct 44	Koch, Karl	5. FJD
6 Oct 44	Gast, Robert	2. FJD	10 May 40	Koch, Walter	1. FJD
14 June 41	Genz, Alfred	7. FJD	9 June 44	Koch, Willi	1. FJD
19 Sept 43	Gerlach, Heinrich	XI. Fliegerkorps	8 Feb 45	Koenig, Franz-Heinz	FPzGD 2 'HG'
14 June 41	Gericke, Walter	7. FJD	7 Feb 45	Koepsel, Herbert	FPzGD 2 'HG'
29 Oct 44	Germer, Ernst	1. FJD	28 Feb 45	Krappmann, Heinrich	FsPzKorps 'HG'
13 Sept 44	Gerstner, Siegfried	2. FJD	9 June 44	Kratzert, Rudolf	1. FJD
28 Apr 45	Gersteuer, Gunther	FstGBrig 12	30 Nov 44	Kraus, Rupert	FPzD 'HG'
24 May 40	Görtz, Helimuth	1. FJD	9 June 44	Krink, Heinz	1. FJD
6 Oct 41	Graf, Rudolf	FlaRegt 'HG'	21 Aug 41	Kroh, Hans	1. FJD
8 Apr 44	Grassmel, Franz	1. FJD	20 Jan 45	Kroymanns, Wilhelm	4. FJD
9 June 44	Gröschke, Kurt	1. FJD	29 Feb 44	Kühne, Martin	2. FJD
29 Oct 44	Grünewald, Georg	FstGBrig 12	30 Nov 44	Kuhlwilm, Wilhelm	FPzGD 2 'HG'
			5 Sept 44	Kulp, Karl	FPzGD 2 'HG'
			18 Nov 44	Kurz, Rudolf	4. FJD
			18 Nov 44	Langemeyer, Karl	FSanitäts
			10 Oct 44	Lehmann, Hans-Georg	FPzD 'HG'
			17 Apr 45	Leitenberger, Helmut	FPzD 'HG'
			8 Aug 44	Lepkowski, Erich	2. FJD

Left: Major Gericke led II./FJR6 in an airborne attack on the Italians near Monte Rotondo, 9 September 1943.

Far Left: Leutnant Eckel commanded 14./FJR4 at Cassino 19 March 1944. He personally knocked out three tanks and the rest of his company another 17 of NZ 20th Armoured Division.

2 Feb 45	Liebing, Walter	8. FJD	19 Feb 45	Schirner, Lothar	FsPzKorps 'HG'
26 Mar 45	Lippe, Hans	FPzD 'HG'	11 June 44	Schlemm, Alfred	1. FsKorps
31 Oct 44	Mager, Rolf	2. FJD	6 Oct 44	Schmid, Fritz-Wilhelm	FPzD 'HG'
15 Jan 45	Majer, Hans von	FPzJagdBn	21 May 43	Schmid, Joseph	FPzD 'HG'
31 Oct 44	Marscholek, Hans	5. FJD	24 May 40	Schmidt, Herbert	1. FJD
14 June 41	Meindl, Eugen	7. Flieger-Div	5 Apr 44	Schmidt, Werner	1. FJD
12 May 40	Meissner, Joachim	1. FJD	21 June 43	Schreiber, Kurt	FPzD 'HG'
9 June 44	Menges, Otto	1. FJD	20 June 43	Graf v d Schulenburg, Wolf-Werner	1. FJD
6 Dec 44	Mertins, Gerhard	5. FJD	24 May 40	Schulz, Karl-Lothar	1. FJD
30 Apr 45	Methner, Gerhard	6. FJD	21 Aug 41	Schuster, Erich	7. Flieger-Div
8 Apr 44	Meyer, Heinz	1. FJD	24 May 40	Schwarzmann, Aifred	1. FJD
17 Sept 43	Meyer, Elimar	XI. Fliegerkorps	28 Feb 45	Schweim, Heinz-Herbert	FPzD 'HG'
9 May 45	Meyer-Schewe, Friedrich	FPzErsatzBrig 'HG'	30 Sept 44	Sempert, Gunther	1. FJD
9 Jan 45	Milch, Werner	Granatwerfer-LehrBn	24 Oct 44	Sniers, Hubert	5. FJD
18 May 43	Mitschke, Gerd	1. FJD	28 Apr 45	Stecken, Albert	8. FJD
24 June 44	Necker, Hanns-Horst von	FPzD 'HG'	30 Nov 44	Steets Konrad	FPzD 'HG'
9 June 44	Neuhoff, Karl	1. FJD	28 Apr 45	Stehle, Werner	FstGBrig 12
21 Aug 41	Neumann, Heinrich	7. Flieger-Div	9 July 41	Stentzler, Edgar	7. Flieger-Div
18 Mar 42	Orth, Heinrich	7. Flieger-Div	30 Sept 44	Stephanie, Kurt	3. FJD
18 Nov 44	Paul, Hugo	7. FJD	16 May 43	Straehler-Pohl, Gunther	FBrig Ramcke
29 Oct 44	Peitsch, Herbert	2. FJD	18 Oct 44	Stronk, Wolfram	FPzD 'HG'
5 Sept 44	Pietzonka, Erich	2. FJD	30 Nov 44	Stuchlik, Werner	FPzD 'HG'
30 Nov 44	Plapper, Albert	FPzD 'HG'	12 May 40	Student, Karl	7. FJD
24 May 40	Prager, Fritz	1. FJD	9 July 41	Sturm, Alfred	1. FJD
30 April 45	Probst, Heinz	FsPzKorps 'HG'	9 July 41	Süssmann, Wilhelm	7. FJD
5 Apr 44	Quednow, Fritz	FPzD 'HG'	5 Apr 44	Tannert, Kari	2 FJD
23 Feb 45	Rademann, Emil	FPzD 'HG'	14 June 41	Teusen, Hans	1. FJD
21 Aug 41	Ramcke, Bernhard-Hermann	7. Flieger-Div	30 Sept44	Thor, Hans	FPzD 'HG'
9 June 44	Rammelt, Siegfried	1. FJD	29 May 40	Tietjen, Cord	1. FJD
10 May 43	Rapraeger, Ernst-Willi	Barenthin	3 Oct 44	Timm, Erich-	4. FJD
28, 43	Rebholz, Robert	FPzD 'HG'	14 June 41	Toschka, Rudolf	7. Flieger-Div
13 Sept 44	Reinighaus, Adolf	2. FJD	9 July 41	Trebes, Horst-	7. Flieger-Div
31 Oct 44	Renisch, Paul-Ernst	1. FJD	24 May 40	Trettner, Heinz	7. FJD
9 June 44	Rennecke, Rudolf	1. FJD	6 Dec 44	Tschierschwitz, Gerhard	FPzD 'HG'
6 Dec 44	Renz, Joachim	FPzD 'HG'	30 April 45	Trotz, Herbert	FestGR Breslau
24 Mar 45	Richter, Heinz	5. FJD	29 Oct 44	Uhlig, Alexander	2. FJD
9 May 45	Riedel, Gerd	2. FJD	30 Sept 44	Veth, Kurt	1. FJD
15 May 40	Ringler, Helmut	1. FJD	24 Jan 42	Wagner, Helmut	1. FJD
9 July 41	Roon, Arnold von	1. FJD	30 Nov 44	Wallhauser, Heinz	FPzD 'HG'
12 Nov 41	Rossmann, Karl	FlaRegt 'HG'	24 May 40	Walther, Erich	1. FJD
28 Feb 45	Sander, Walter	5. FJD	24 Oct 44	Wangerin, Friedrich-Wilhelm	III./FJR 3
18 Oct 44	Sandrock, Hans	FPzD 'HG'	21 Aug 41	Welskop, Heinrich	1. FJD
22 Feb 42	Sassen, Bruno	1. FJD	9 June 44	Werner, Walter	1. FJD
12 May 40	Schacht, Gerhard	1. FJD	28 Jan 45	Wimmer, Johann	FPzErsatzRegt 'HG'
12 May 40	Schächter, Martin	1. FJD	18 May 44	Witte, Heinrich	FPzD 'HG'
8 Aug 44	Schäfer, Heinrich	4./FJR 5	5 Feb 44	Wittig, Hans-Karl	1. FJD
21 June 43	Scheid, Johannes	FPzD 'HG'	10 May 40	Witzig, Rudolf	1. FJD
6 Oct 44	Schimpf, Richard	3. FJD	9 June 44	Zahn, Hilmar	1. FJD
5 Sept 44	Schimpke, Horst	1. FJD	28 Apr 45	Zander, Wolfgang	FPzGD 2 'HG'
14 June 41	Schirmer, Gerhard	1. FJD	15 May 40	Zierach, Otto	1. FJD

Above: Generalmajor Schmalz commander of the Hermann Göring Fallschirm-Panzer-Division at Anzio.

Above: General Fritz Morzic was the Ju 52 Assault Transport Group commander for the invasion of Holland, May 1940.

Below: Oberst Heilmann commanded FJR 3 at Cassino and was awarded the Knight's Cross with Oakleaves.

Below: Generalleutnant Richard Heidrich was commander of 1. FJD at Cassino.

POSTWAR

Above: Postwar Bundeswehr 1.FJD jumping from a Luftwaffe Noratlas transport.

In 1955, with the sanction of the NATO Allies and the three-power occupiers of West Germany (USA, Britain, France), it was decided to set up the West German Armed Forces (Bundeswehr) comprising Navy, Air Force, and Army (the Bundesheer) as an integrated part of NATO. The planners decided that an airborne brigade, and an associated airborne school and depot, should be part of the new Bundesheer.

In 1956 the first elements of the new formation were recruited from officers, NCOs and men who had been in the wartime 7. Flieger, the idea being that these should form the backbone of the new force in command, instructional, and administrative roles. Units for recruiting purposes were set up at Ellwangen, Kempten, Esslingen, and Böblingen. The first young volunteers were then recruited and all of them, including the wartime veterans, were then moved to Augsburg to carry out comprehensive parachute training with the 11th Airborne Division of the US Army which was based there at that time.

It was decided early on that the brigade should be expanded to division size and from 1 January 1957, it was designated 1. Luftlandedivision (1st Airborne Division). The first divisional commander was Oberst von Baer who had been Airborne Panzer Corps chief of staff in World War II. The new division was based at Becelaere Barracks, Esslingen. During that year jump training was taken over by the airborne division's own training school, starting in April. First deployment of the still under-strength division was in the autumn exercises of 1957 and just before that Generalmajor Kroh became divisional commander. He had been the wartime commander of the 2nd Parachute Division.

By April 1958 the division was up to full strength and was declared combat-ready to NATO standards and took its place in the order of battle of NATO Land Forces Central Europe. In the NATO exercises that year the division operated for the first time with other NATO airborne units. In 1959 the division was expanded to comprise two full brigades, 25. and 26. Fallschimjägerbrigaden, the latter being the newer formation. The same year's exercises saw the biggest drop yet, in battalion strength at Heuberg. In 1960–61 the various units of the division moved to newer barracks, the 26th Brigade to Bergzabern, Lebach, and Zweibrücken, and 25th Brigade to Calw and Nagold. Divisional and support units moved to Bruchsal and Stetten. In 1961 the division took part in exercises in France and also cross-operated in Germany with US airborne units, while German and US personnel were seconded between the 1st Airborne and US airborne divisions for experience. There was a good degree of standardisation with US airborne techniques and the US Army T10 parachute also became the standard German airborne parachute. Some items of equipment were common, too.

In 1962 Generalmajor Gericke became divisional commander. He was a veteran of Crete (where he won the Knight's Cross) and he had also served in Italy (where he was awarded Oak Leaves to the cross). Oberst Hermann, wartime commander of the 9th Parachute Division, became commander of the airborne and air transport training school. In 1964 divisional HQ was set up at Eichelberg Barracks in Bruchsal. Divisional and support troops included military police, engineer, anti-tank, air defence (flak), signal, medical, maintenance, transport and supply companies. All personnel were trained as parachutists.

Instead of the old Ju 52, the standard airborne transport aircraft of the 1950s was the French-built Noratlas which was supplied to the Luftwaffe. This was of the twin-boom, centre fuselage pod configuration much favoured for tactical transport aircraft in the 1950s. In the late 1960s the Noratlas was replaced by the C-160 Transall, a Franco-German design similar to the Lockheed Hercules. In the 1960s the use of helicopters in the 'vertical envelopment' role was introduced and an Army Aviation Corps wing was attached to the division equipped with American-built H-34, CH-53, and UH-1 Huey helicopters.

The post-war German parachutist was awarded a cloth 'jump badge' on qualifying which was in simplified style but on the lines of the wartime 'jump badge'. This is worn on the right breast pocket. The formation sign of the division was a white parachute on a blue background, worn on the left sleeve on the uniform but also carried on some vehicles and equipment. The historic 7. Flieger name was not perpetuated even though the original key personnel were all World War II parachute veterans, and the post-war German parachute forces were, and remain, an Army (Bundesheer) commitment. While the tradition of fighting efficiency has been retained, the post-war doctrine is, of course, not linked in any way to the Third Reich era.

Below: Airlanding troops of 1. FJD during exercises in 1970.

ASSESSMENT

Above: Composite propaganda photograph purporting to show the landing on Crete in 1941. While it conveys a good impression of a German parachute landing, it is obviously a montage. By Crete the parachutes weren't white, but drab.

The German airborne troops were truly pioneers, for though they were not the first to exploit the idea of using aircraft to bring military men into action from the air – that honour went to the Russians – they were the first to develop the idea to its logical conclusion after Russian efforts were stalled by Stalin's military purges of 1937–39. All the methods of landing sticks of men from the air, complete with equipment, the use of gliders, follow up air-landing components, and even the means of bringing in heavier equipment by air, were all first tackled and developed by the Germans. That they got it right, or largely right given the technology of the time, may be judged by the fact that when the British and Americans formed their own airborne forces in the early years of the war they used the Luftwaffe airborne forces and organisation largely as a pattern to copy, and the copying extended even to the smocks which are still the familiar garb of all military paratroops.

While the German paratroops were arguably the keenest and most professional of all German military forces, second to none in bravery, enthusiasm, fighting qualities, elan and team spirit, they suffered tactically by being the pioneer users of this form of warfare.

Their greatest limitation was the mode of parachute delivery, based on the early Italian Salvatore method, whereby the canopy shrouds were brought to an attachment point in the harness behind the parachutist's back. Therefore he could not reach the shrouds and achieve any kind of directional control. This meant that drops had to be made in calm weather. Even in these conditions it was only too easy for a drop to go wrong, with men being scattered over a wide area or blown well off the intended drop zone.

The parachute design also meant that small arms and ammunition, as well as heavier support weapons, had to be dropped in separate containers (*Waffenhalter*), which added another factor of vulnerability. First, the containers had to be located by the units they were intended for once on the ground, and could just as easily be scattered like the men, if not lost altogether in trees, rivers, etc. Second, any sort of organised ground resistance, as at Crete and Dombås (Norway), could stop or delay the men from reaching their containers and so render them largely impotent as a fighting unit. To some extent this was partly overcome by hardened veterans who jumped with their small arms, against regulations, but the problem was never solved throughout the whole period of German airborne operations, and there was hardly any drop where some problem, large or small, did not arise with scattered men and lost containers.

British and American airborne forces learnt from observing this German experience and adopted parachutes with shoulder harnesses which allowed a degree of directional control by the parachutist, plus a weapons/kit pack which dropped with the parachutist, a huge advance over the German method. By contrast the British and American use of gliders was somewhat crude and basic as a way of getting air-landing troops into area, not always safely. They hardly ever used gliders with the great precision perfected by the Germans, with a skill and daring never equalled or attempted since.

Like Rommel's *Afrika Korps*, the German airborne forces were relatively free from Nazi political interference or indoctrination, possibly because, like the *Afrika Korps*, they were something of a 'sideshow' in the eyes of both the Wehrmacht high command and the Nazi hierarchy. Political 'commissars' and functionaries were absent except that Göring was a benign patron and supporter in his capacity as Luftwaffe chief, so was happy to bask in any honours and successes the airborne forces achieved.

Above: Recovering equipment from a container— easily lost during the drop or difficult to recover, this would be a major limitation to all German parachute operations.

Though the German airborne forces existed for only seven years up to the end of World War II it took only the first year of war for the most important lesson to be learned – that in general airborne drops have only limited potential to hold an objective. It is vitally important to relieve them with heavier forces as soon as possible if setbacks are not to result. Even though the Germans learnt this in their earliest operations, in Norway and the Low Countries in 1940, they tended to overlook it very expediently in later operations, notably at Crete, which nearly ended in large scale disaster and changed the attitude of Hitler and the high command completely when it came to the use of airborne troops. Needless to say the British and Americans had to learn these same lessons the hard way, as Arnhem memorably demonstrated. Looked at half a century on, it seems that the earliest German notion of using small groups of airborne troops as shock troops to take specific objectives by surprise – as at Eben Emael – was always the best way to use them. Most operations based on this principle worked, and those with more ambitious objectives like securing large airfields or areas of ground most often failed. Nothing seems to have changed in this respect over the years.

The bravery, dedication, courage and camaraderie of the German airborne forces became the stuff of legend and it is interesting to note that, even in the final year of the war when most units were made up of new and hastily trained recruits or men transferred from ordinary Luftwaffe units, they quickly lived up to the airborne tradition of team work, initiative, and resolve, taking their cue from the early veterans who still served as the backbone of most divisions. Disparate as the later divisions were, Student, their commander, could contemplate with pride that his original 7. Flieger-Division of 1939 had grown to ten divisions, three corps and an airborne army by 1945, and without exception all these formations fought well and proudly to the end, maintaining the zeal and determination that had characterised the German airborne forces from the time of the first volunteers for the service.

Writing in 1961, Kurt Student, then long retired, wrote: 'The first use of a new weapon is always a risk. For the parachute troops this was indeed the case, for there was no previous example to go by. Their first employment in war was truly a "leap in the dark" in every sense of these words. The employment of parachute troops offered then, as it still does today, undreamed of opportunities for far-sighted military leadership. I gave this weighty and serious complex of questions, with the advantages and disadvantages, my special attention, and took the problem damned seriously. It was clear to me that, in airborne operations, there was a thin line separating defeat from victory, as Crete, and even more Arnhem, made quite apparent. Time for organisation and training was much too short – only 14 months when we started. When I undertook my mission the first lightning flashes of the coming war were already on the horizon.'

REFERENCE

BIBLIOGRAPHY

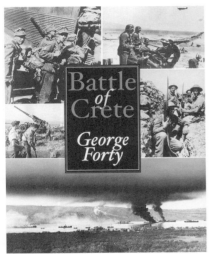

Battle of Crete George Forty, Ian Allan Publishing, 2001.
A recent account of the battle with numerous illustrations and personal stories. It is particularly good on the German invasion, by air and sea, and the Royal Navy operations that destroyed the latter.

The German Paratroops (UK title)/*Fallschirmjäger* (German title), Rudolf Bohmler and Werner Haupt, Almark Publishing (UK)/Verlag Hans-Henning Podzun (Germany), 1971.
A very comprehensive history of the wartime and post-war period organisation and operations of the German parachute troops in both the German and English languages. The authors were wartime members of 7. Flieger and write with unique knowledge. The book also contains a fine collection of pictures, many of them rare and not seen elsewhere, taken from regimental or personal sources in many cases. There is also a very comprehensive listing of all unit commanding officers, staff officers, award winners, and orders of battle from which some of the details are included in this present book.

Storming Eagles, James Lucas, Arms & Armour 1988.
Another comprehensive history with much extra information on equipment, orders of battle, and some campaign maps. Noted military author James Lucas had combat experience against German paratroops in North Africa and Italy and writes much from personal experience and wartime knowledge. This is a very good single volume book on the subject.

Invasion of England 1940, Peter Schenk, Conway Maritime Press, 1990, (originally published in German as *Landung in England*, Oberbaum Verlag, 1987).
This very detailed and comprehensive book describes every aspect of the planned Operation Sea Lion in 1940, including good coverage of the airborne aspects and planning.

The Lost Battle, Crete 1941, Callum Macdonald, Macmillan 1993.
A highly detailed and thoroughly researched book on the battle of Crete with major coverage of the 7. Flieger part in capturing the island. It also includes much on the political background to the campaign and some history of the birth and training of 7. Flieger and its commitments before Crete. There is good coverage, too, of key personalities.

Weapons and Equipment of the German Fallschirmtruppe, 1935–45, Alex Buchner, Schiffer Publishing 1996.
Useful pictorial coverage with supporting text on all the small arms, heavy weapons, and associated equipment used by the German airborne troops in battle.

Fallschirmjäger in Action, Uwe Feist and Norman Harms, Squadron Signal, 1973.
An excellent collection of photographs of German airborne operations, together with drawings of uniform details, badges and insignia, plus centre-spread artwork of uniform variations. All illustrations have good informative captions.

Uniforms and Insignia of the Luftwaffe, Volume 1, Brian L. Davis, Arms & Armour, 1991.
This very comprehensive reference work, profusely illustrated and detailed, covers all Luftwaffe uniforms and badges, but includes all the paratroop uniform items as well, and is the authoritative book as far as precise details and specifications of uniform clothing are concerned.

Crete was my Waterloo, Neville Chesterton, Janus, 1995.
While this book covers the whole war period it includes chapters giving the author's experience of fighting – and being captured – in the Crete campaign, a good impression from a private soldier.

German Airborne Troops 1939–45, Bruce Quarrie, Osprey, 1983.
This useful book gives a necessarily brief account of the wartime history of the German airborne troops but has good colour plates showing all the uniform variations over the course of the war, plus good details of weapons, uniforms, and equipment, and a good selection of pictures.

Ultra and Mediterranean Strategy 1941-45, Bennett, Ralph, Hamish Hamilton 1989
This book has a particularly good account of the way Ultra intercepts were used and interpreted by the British and how they affected the defence of Crete during the German airborne invasion.

Signal No 12, 1944
This contains a good account, with maps and photographs, of the action on Crete.

INTERNET SITES

http://www.feldgrau.com/
This is probably the most comprehensive site currently on the Web dealing with the German Army before and during World War II. Well-written and researched, and an intriguing in-depth interview with a *Grossdeutschland* veteran, too.

http://www.tankclub.agava.ru/sign/sign.shtml
Russian-language site with excellent illustrations of the tactical signs of the German Armyhttp://www.generals.dk
This is an private project trying to provide biographical data on the army generals of World War II, including many German generals.

http://www.eliteforcesofthethirdreich.com/
Useful information on Fallschirmjäger and associated units

http://www.geocities.com/~pkeller/fj_index.htm
Website of *Fallschirmjäger Regiment 6* — a US living history group that honors the military service and sacrifices of all World War II veterans, specifically the German paratroopers of World War II.

http://www.eagle19.freeserve.co.uk/index.html
Website of Greg Way aimed at the enthusiast, to give an outlook on nine years of the Fallschirmjäger from 1936–45.

http://www.greendevils.com/
The website of the *Fallschirm Pionier Bataillon* reenactment group, part of Kampfgruppe Martz, a kampfgruppe comprised of our unit and the Luftlande Sturmregiment. A member of the W2HPG, it attends events on the east coast of the United States.

The fort at Eben Emael is still in existence and is now a museum. The website (http://www.fort-eben emael.be/English/Frame4/10_may_1940.htm) includes detailed coverage of the battle.

The battle of Crete is well-covered on the Web, including an excellent section on the New Zealand History net (http://www.nzhistory.net.nz/Gallery/crete/index.htm) giving details of the New Zealand side of the battle

British-forces.com has a substantial entry on the battle (http://british-forces.com/world_war2/Campaigns /Crete.html). There are museums about the battle of Crete and the occupation of the island by the Germans — particularly the Municipal Museum of the Battle of Crete and National Resistance in Heraklion on the Doukos Bofor and Meramelou road (telephone 3081246554) is on http://www.culture.gr/4/42/421/42103n/e42103nl.html (or http://www.heraklion-city.gr/english/mus-mah-en.htm); it also has links to the Cretan Naval Museum.

Information on Fallschirmjäger in Africa can be sourced at: http://www.ww2battles.com/afrikakorps/dak/fallschirm jager.htm. This site covers everything to do with the Afrika Korps including details on the Ramcke Fallschirm Brigade. A biography of Ramcke himself (in French) can be found on http://www.1939-45.org/bios/ramcke.htm

The battles at Monte Cassino have a number of sites including http://www.accessweb.com/users/rbereznicki/over.html-ssi. This covers the battle, as well as having many interesting links; it is part of the Wargamer's ring.

SS-Sturmbannführer Otto Skorzeny is well descibed in a biography at http://www.forces70.freeserve.co.uk/Waffen %20SS%Text+ Images/kschol.../skorzeny.ht. A link from this site studies the rescue of Mussolini from the Gran Sasso.

There are a number of wargaming sites, some online some giving wargame information, that cover German Fallschirmjäger, including:
http://home.earthlink.net/~jabo3rdfj/3rdFallschirmjager/ Home/HQ.html
This is an online wargaming site, the Generalkomando der 3rd. Fallschirmjager Division.
http://motiondigital.com/pccs/fallton. htm
Profile of the Fallschirmjäger with weapon value information

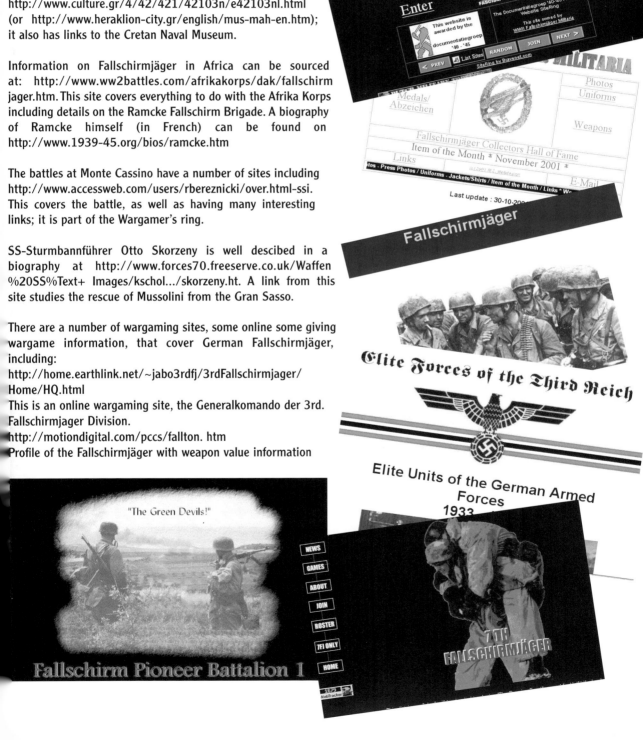

INDEX

Albert Canal, 18, 20, 24, 25, 27, 62
Altmann, Gustav, 26, 84
Anzio, 21, 87

Badges and insignia, 73–75
Balloons, 7, 9
Belgium, 20, 24, 27, 31, 55, 66
Bräuer, Bruno, 8, 9, 11, 16, 34, 46, 85
Brest, 61, 63, 82

Canea, 37, 41, 44
Cassino, Monte, 21, 50, 53, 56, 58, 83, 85, 86, 87, 94
Corinth Canal, 20, 35, 35–38, 39, 56
Crete, 17, 20, 36, 37, 38–44, 48, 56, 70, 72, 73, 76, 77, 79, 82, 83, 89, 90, 91, 92, 93, 94, 95

Delica, Egon, 25, 26, 84
Denmark, 18, 20, 22
DFS 230 glider, 10, 25, 43, 50, 78, 79

Eben Emael, 18, 20, 24–26, 27, 28, 30, 34, 50, 80, 91, 94
Erdmann, Wolfgang, 62, 64, 85

Freyberg, Bernard, 39, 44

Gericke, Walther, 22, 46, 53, 62, 66, 84, 85, 89
German units:
  Fallschirmjäger units—1. Fallschirm-Armee, 21, 60, 62, 85; 1. FJD, 21, 49, 53, 56, 63, 66, 73, 74, 83, 84, 85, 86, 87, 88, 89; 2. FJD, 21, 49, 51, 53, 56, 58, 63, 66, 73, 74, 83, 85, 86; 3. FJD, 56, 58, 66, 85, 86; 4. FJD, 21, 58, 63, 66, 74, 75, 83, 85, 86; 5. FJD, 56, 62, 63, 66, 85, 86; 6. FJD, 62, 66, 86; 7. FJD, 44, 62, 63, 66, 85, 86; 8. FJD, 62, 66, 86; 9. FJD, 21, 61, 62, 66, 85; 10. FJD, 62, 66; 11. FJD, 62, 66; I. Fliegerkorps, 58; II. Fallschirmkorps, 57, 82; II. Fliegerkorps, 58; 7. Flieger-Division, 10, 11, 12, 14, 16, 17, 18, 19, 20, 22, 26, 27, 28, 30, 31, 34, 35, 39, 40, 41, 44, 46, 48, 66, 75, 82, 83, 85, 86, 88, 91, 92; VIII. Fliegerkorps, 40; XI. Fliegerkorps, 35, 38, 39, 44, 53; 22nd Air Landing Division, 18, 27, 28, 30, 31, 34, 35, 74; Fallschirmjäger Brigade Ramcke, 20, 72, 73, 74, 86; Fallschirmjäger-Sturmregiment, 17, 31, 35, 39; Fallschirm-Panzer-Division/Korps 'Hermann Göring', 14, 21, 51, 57, 58, 61, 85, 86, 87; FJR 1, 8, 10, 11, 12, 18, 20, 21, 24, 27, 28, 34, 41, 43, 44, 46, 47, 49, 56, 66; FJR 2, 12, 21, 27, 28, 34, 35,

36, 41, 44, 46, 56, 61, 66; FJR 3, 34, 36, 41, 44, 46, 47, 49, 50, 52, 56, 66, 86, 87; FJR 4, 47, 50, 66, 85; FJR 5, 20, 50, 58, 66, 85, 86; FJR 6, 21, 52, 63, 66, 85; FJR 7, 21, 44, 56, 64; FJR 8, 58, 66; FJR 9, 58, 66; FJR 10, 58, 66; FJR 11, 66; FJR 12, 66; ; FJR 13, 62, 66; FJR 14, 62, 66; FJR 15, 62, 66; FJR 16, 66; FJR 17, 62, 66; FJR 18, 62, 66; FJR 19, 66; FJR 20, 66; FJR 21, 66; FJR 25, 62, 66; FJR 26, 62, 66; FJR 27, 62, 66; FJR 28, 66; FJR 29, 66; FJR 30, 66; FJR 37, 62, 66; FJR 38, 62, 66; FJR 39, 62, 66; Kampfgruppe Bräuer, 34; Kampfgruppe Stentzler, 34; Luftflotte 2, 18, 82; Luftlande Geschwader, 17, 78; Luftlandekorps, 19; Luftlande-Regiment Feldherrnhalle, 10, 11; Regiment General Göring, 8, 9, 10; LLStR, 39, 41, 43, 44, 46, 53, 57, 94; StuG-Brigade XI, 63; StuG-Brigade XI; Stürmabteilung Koch, 18, 24, 25, 29; Test Section Friedrichshafen, 18 Other units—3. Panzergrenadier Division, 53, 75; 5. Gebirgs Division, 20, 40, 41, 46; 100. Gebirgs Division, 44, 46; 34. Gebirgs Division, 24; Afrika Korps, 49, 50, 83, 90, 91, 95; AR22, 19; Eighteenth Army, 28; Fourteenth Army, 58; XLIX Corps, 28; Brandenburg Division, 44; IR16, 19; IR47, 19, 28; IR65, 19; Landespolizeigruppe General Göring, 8; SS Leibstandarte Adolf Hitler Regiment 28
Göring, Hermann, 7, 8, 10, 11, 30, 38, 56, 73, 91
Gran Sasso, 21, 50, 94
Gustav Line, 56

Heidrich, Richard, 9, 10, 16, 46, 47, 49, 66, 83, 84, 85, 87
Heilmann, Ludwig, 52, 66, 85, 86
Heraklion, 37, 40, 41, 44, 92
Hitler, 9, 11, 12, 14, 16, 18, 22, 25, 27, 28, 30, 31, 34, 35, 38, 44, 49, 56, 91
Holland, 18, 20, 26–30, 31, 32, 34, 54, 62, 76, 87, 91

Junkers Ju 52, 8, 10, 12, 17, 19, 22, 23, 24, 25, 28, 30, 31, 32, 34, 36, 38, 40, 41, 42, 48, 56, 68, 73, 75, 76, 77, 79, 87, 89

Kesselring, Albert, 7, 8, 10, 18, 29, 31, 49, 82,
Koch, 18, 27, 44, 46, 50, 85
Kroh, Hans, 8, 61, 66, 75, 84, 85, 88

Leros, 21

Maas, River, 21, 24, 26, 28, 63
Maleme, 37, 39, 40, 41, 43
Meindl, Eugen, 31, 35, 41, 46, 56, 83, 84, 86
Meissner, Joachim, 26, 27, 28, 84

Milch, Erhard, 7, 10
Mitchell, Billy, 6
Morzik, 16, 19, 87
Moscow Air Days, 6
Munich Agreement, 11
Mussolini 21, 50. 94

Narvik, 18, 20, 22, 24
Normandy, 21, 56, 58, 62
Norway, 18, 20, 22, 24, 28, 90, 91

OKW, 10, 36
Operations: Attila, 34–35; Barbarossa, 38, 40, 44; Flying Dutchman, 40; Hannibal, 39; Mercury, 38; Sea Lion, 30–34; 92; Torch (allied), 59; Weserübung, 18

Parachutes: RZ1, 8; RZ16, 15; RZ20, 10, 15, 83
Petersen, 44, 82, 83
Poland, 12–14, 18
Putzier, Richard, 19, 30, 31

Reitsch, Hanna, 10
Retimo, 37, 40, 41, 44
Rhineland, 21, 63, 66
Ringel, General, 41, 44, 46
Ritterkreuzträger, 82–84
Rotundo, Monte, 21, 85

Salerno, 53
Schmidt, Herbert, 22, 23, 29, 84
Schram, 10, 16, 66
Schulz, Karl-Lothar, 8, 27, 56, 64, 66, 84, 86
Sicily, 21, 49, 79
Sponeck, Graf von, 19, 28
Stendal, 8, 9, 11, 15, 16, 24, 82
Stentzler, Edgar, 41, 44, 46, 86
Student, Kurt, 7, 8, 9, 10, 11, 12, 16, 18, 19, 25, 28, 29, 30, 34, 35, 38, 40, 41, 44, 46, 49, 53, 62, 82, 83, 84, 86, 91
Sturm, Alfred, 46, 86
Suda Bay, 37, 38, 39, 40, 41, 43,
Süssmann, Wilhelm, 35, 36, 39, 41, 46, 83, 86

Tietjen, 28, 86
Trettner, Heinz, 10, 35, 46, 58, 66, 83, 84, 86
Tukhachevski, Mikhail, 7
Tunisia, 20, 48, 50, 78

Udet, Ernst, 10
Uniforms, 68–73

Walther, Erich, 8, 22, 28, 66, 84, 86
Wavell, Archibald, 7, 39
Wever, Walther, 7, 8
Witzig, Rudolf, 24, 25, 27, 28, 50, 66, 86
World War I, 6

Zahn, Hilmar, 9, 86